Home Cooked Culture...

Wisconsin through Recipes

Edited by Terese Allen
Compiled by Choua Ly

Contents

Appetizers

Finnish Squeaky Cheese Sauce	2
Mushroom Tart	4
Appetizer Quiche	5
Swissconsin Cheese Toasts	6
Rueben Dip	7
Gouda Fondue with Beer or Wine	8
White Girl Salsa	8.1

Pancakes and Crepes

Palacinky (Slovak Crepes)	9
Norwegian Lefse	10
Kropsua (Oven Pancakes)	11
Norwegian Lefse	12
Aunt Yetta's Potato Leeks	14
Crepes	15
Great Grandmas Potato Pancakes	16
Pancakes	17

Soups

Cherry Dumpling Soup	19
Wild Game Chili	20
Wild Rice Soup	21
Creamed Spring Borsch (Beet Soup)	22
Denzin Manke Cherry Soup	23
Hungarian Goulash Soup	24
Beerwurst Soup	25
Indian Corn Soup	27
Sherried Cheese Soup	28
Chicken Bouyan (or Booyah)	30

Side Dishes

Sweet Sour Cabbage	32
Dandelion Greens	33
Norma Cashin's Dill Pickles	34
Sichuan Noodles	35
Plum Dumplings	36
Corn Mush	37
Busia's Potato Cake	38

Main Dishes

Prime Rib Wild Mallard Canvas Back	39
Tamales	40
Chiles Rellenos (Stuffed Peppers) with Tomato Soup	42
Pasties	44
Cowley's Canned Venison	46
Goblaki (Stuffed Cabbage Rolls)	48
Stuffed Pumpkins	49
Floisgrad	50
Geschnetzletz	51
Chalber Balleli (Veal Balls)	52
Friday Fish Fry	53
Pork Chops with Cranberry-Barbecue Glaze	55
Spanakopita (Spinach Pie)	56
Home-Cured Beef Tongue	57
Rouladen	58
Chicken Paprika	59
Smoked Turkey and Cranberry Gourmet Pizza	60
Spanakopitas	62
Wild Rice with Italian Sausage	64
Pijani Saran (Drunken Carp)	65
Sarma (Stuffed Caggabe and Sauerkraut)	66
Rouladen (Stuffed Rolled Beef Slices)	68
Italian Chicken	70
Bratwurst A la Vern	71
Pork Chops with Knackwurst	72

Breads, Rolls and Muffins

Sekahiivaleipa (Mixed Grain Loaves)	73
Cinnamon Rhubarb Muffins	
Irish Soda Bread	
Pogasca (Biscuits)	
Never Fail Rolls	
Cannery Corn Bread	

Cookies and Bars

Sidonka's Slovak Honey Cookies	
Viennese Cut-out Cookies	
Strul (Waffle Cookie)	
Oatmeal Cookies	
Latvian "Piparkukas" (Peppercakes)	
Cranberry Slices	
Sandbakkelse	
Belgian "Boonohs"	

Desserts and Pastries

Bratislava Apple Strudel	
Easy Low-fat Microwave Norwegiar Rommegrot	
Nottekake (Nut Cake)	
Norwegian Kransekake (Norwegian Almond Ring Cake)	
Rich Coffee Cake and Filling	
Easy Flan	
Passover Chocolate Cake	
Chocolate Bundt Cake	
Doughnuts	
Point Bock Beer Cake	
Sour Cream Pie	
Nodji's Cranberry Tassies	
Jim's Favorite Cranberry Pie	
Struesel Rasberry-Cherry Pie	
O & H Danish Kringle	
Pita iz Ananasa (Pineapple Pita)	
Ida Denzin's Kuchen	
Rosky-filled Crescents	
Cranberry Pie	
Orahnjaca (Nut Roll)	

photographical index	

Foreword

The Arts Board publishing a cookbook?

These traditional family recipes have been collected from the participants and staff of the Wisconsin Folklife Festival. This festival is the largest single project carried out by the Wisconsin Arts Board. Produced in collaboration with the Wisconsin Sesquicentennial Commission and the Smithsonian Institution, the folklife festival highlights Wisconsin's traditions in music, dance, crafts, occupational and recreational skills and foodways. Such an ambitious undertaking in the area of folk arts would have seemed impossible when I started the program 15 years ago.

In 1983, like a number of other academically trained folklorists in the 80s, I found a career opportunity as the folk arts coordinator in my states arts agency, the Wisconsin Arts Board. The Arts Board had a great deal of experience dealing with the world of the fine arts but was seeking to broaden its area of concern to include the folk arts.

Typical of the meeting of any two worlds, at first there were communication difficulties. To me the fine art world's focus on a particular set of defined artistic genres, like classical music, painting, sculpture, modern dance, seemed narrow and arbitrary. To my arts world peers my acceptance of so many forms of traditional expressive behavior, from customizing cars to canning vegetables seemed vague and without standards. Over time, I learned to appreciate the priorities and concerns of performing arts presenters, touring artists, museums and galleries, theatre and dance companies, arts educators, writers, composers, painters and sculptors. For their part, the Arts Board grasped and embraced my notion of supporting culturally grounded expressive pursuits that go beyond the established arts genres.

The issue of whether the Arts Board should be concerned about foodways came up early in my tenure. An application for a folk arts apprenticeship involving tapping maple trees and making maple sugar came in from the Red Cliff Ojibwe reservation in northern Wisconsin. At the board meeting, a member questioned whether the Arts Board should even consider this request. The board seemed reassured and I managed to win approval of the grant when I pointed out that the maple sugar makers have hand-carved wooden molds into which they pour the maple sugar producing little edible sculptural pieces!

At that point the Board still was used to the notion that art had to appeal to two senses only—sight or hearing. It has taken a number of years to reach a mutual understanding. Today the Wisconsin Arts Board is pleased to present Wisconsin's foodways heritage and recognizes that foods are significant aesthetic creations that appeal to the senses of smell, taste and touch (as well as sight and occasionally even hearing).

Foodways are among the most pervasive and lasting forms of folklife. Wisconsinites who may no longer speak the language, sing the songs or fashion the crafts of their immigrant forebears tenaciously hold onto their ancestors' food traditions. Preparing and consuming ethnic food is a powerful mark of ethnic identity. On the other hand, it is also a major way of cross-cultural sharing. Sampling the unique ethnic dishes of other cultures is an ever-popular way of learning about the diverse ways of our neighbors. Furthermore, there are some foods that have become emblematic of Wisconsin and our Midwest region. When Wisconsinites consume brats and beer, cream puffs and cheese curds, maple sugar, pasties, wild rice, cranberries and other regional specialties, it is a common bond that helps define us as denizens of the Badger State.

So try out these recipes, attend food-oriented community events and enjoy the rich heritage of Wisconsin foods.

Richard March, Director
Wisconsin Folklife Festival

A ppetiz e RS...

Wisconsin Through Recipes

Irene Vuorenmaa
Wisconsin Folklife Festival Participant
Rag Rug weaver
Hurley

3 gallons raw farm milk

3/4 c. salt

1 Hansen cheese rennet tablet

2 T. warm water

additional salt (optional)

Finnish Squeaky Cheese

Heat milk to lukewarm on stovetop, stir in salt, and remove milk from heat.

Dissolve rennet tablet in the 2 tablespoons warm water. Add rennet tablet and water to milk. Pour mixture into milk pail. Let it stand at room temperature 1 hour.

Heat top coil (broiler) in electric oven. Move oven rack 10-15 inches from top coil. (You may also use a gas oven.) Place milk pail in large pan filled with hot water to warm the milk. Stir the milk; the cheese will start to form into curds. Scoop the liquid whey off the top a little at a time. Most of the curds will sink to bottom of pail, but if any get caught in your scoop, strain them out and return them to the pail. Also, as the curds form, press down with your hands to form the cheese. This process takes about 1/2 hour.

Press cheese into a 9-by-13-inch cake pan. "Broil" cheese in hot oven until light brown dots form on top, about 20 minutes. Remove pan from oven, place large plate or board over cheese, flip cheese onto plate, then slide cheese back into pan and return it to the oven. Bake the other side until light brown dots form on top.

Remove from oven. Slide or flip the cheese onto a large cutting board. Wet your hands (to keep them cool) then flatten cheese, being careful not to burn your hands. Angle the cutting board to drain excess whey; let stand at room temperature 30 minutes. Flip cheese and drain again, about 20 minutes. Cheese is now ready to eat. Season with additional salt if desired. Refrigerate or freeze any leftovers.

"I created (the recipe). We needed additional recipes for our award winning Gouda and Sweet Swiss. I also took advantage of other products for sale at the Madison Farmers' Market, such as fresh mushrooms, herbs and eggs"
Michelle Krahenbuhl
Wisconsin Folklife Festival Participant
Cheesemaker
Monticello

1 sheet (15 grams) refrigerated unbaked
    pie crust pastry

2 T. butter

2 c. fresh mushrooms

1/4 c. chopped fresh marjoram

1 c. grated sweet-style Swiss cheese

1/2 c. grated Gouda

1/2 c. chopped Canadian bacon

2 eggs beaten

1/2 c. milk

1 T. snipped chives

Optional: additional chopped Canadian
    bacon

fresh marjoram sprigs.

Mushroom Tart

Serves 10

Heat oven to 450 degrees. Using pastry according to directions, ease the sheet into a 9-inch tart pan with removable bottom. Press pastry into flutes on the side of the tart pan and trim the top even with the top of the pan. Do not prick. Cover the pastry with a layer of foil to prevent excessive browning. Bake 8 minutes. Remove foil and continue baking for another 4-5 minutes or until pastry is set and dry. Reduce the oven temperature to 375 F.

Meanwhile, heat butter in large skillet over medium-high heat. Add mushrooms and chopped marjoram; saute until mushrooms are tender and liquid is evaporated, 4-5 minutes. Remove from heat.

Combine sweet-style Swiss, Gouda and chopped Canadian bacon in large bowl. Add mushroom mixture, eggs, milk, and chives. Stir to thoroughly mix. Pour carefully into the partially baked pastry shell. Bake 20 minutes or until set and golden brown. Cool in pan on a wire rack 10-15 minutes. Remove from pan. Cut into wedges and garnish with Canadian bacon and fresh marjoram sprigs, if desired.

Appetizer Quiche

Makes 8-10 appetizer servings

Heat oven to 400 F. Place pie crust on bottom of 9 or 10 inch pie pan or oblong glass baking dish. Arrange sausage over crust; sprinkle cheese on top. Combine milk, eggs, onion, green pepper, and seasonings. Pour over crust. Bake 20-25 minutes, until set. Let stand a few minutes before you cut and serve.

Debra Usinger
(a recipe from "A Friend of Usinger's")
Wisconsin Folklife Festival Participant
Sausage making and cookery
Milwaukee

1 frozen pie crust, slightly thawed

8 oz. Usinger's Little Link pork sausage, browned and sliced

2 c. grated Swiss cheese

3/4 c. milk

4 eggs, lightly beaten

2 T. chopped onion

2 T chopped green pepper

1/2 t. salt

1/2 t. oregano

1/4 t. pepper

Michelle Krahenbuhl
Wisconsin Folklife Festival Participant
Cheesemaker
Monticello

1 T. olive oil

1 large onion, thinly sliced and quartered

1 t. dried rosemary, crushed

1/4 t. salt

1/4 t. freshly ground black pepper

12 slices French baguette (narrow French
   bread)

Dijon mustard

1/2 lb. shredded Emmenthaler cheese

Swissconsin Cheese Toasts

Makes 12 pieces

Heat olive oil in large skillet over medium heat. Add onions and cook 5-10 minutes, stirring occasionally. Reduce heat to medium-low. Continue cooking onions for 15 minutes or until browned and very tender, stirring frequently. Stir in rosemary, salt and pepper. Remove from heat.

Heat oven to 425 F. Line a baking sheet with aluminum foil or parchment paper. Spread bread slices evenly with mustard and top with Emmenthaler. Divide onion mixture evenly over cheese. Place on baking sheet. Bake 10 minutes or until cheese is melted.

Reuben Dip

Heat cream cheese, sour cream, corned beef, Emmenthaler and sauerkraut in a small saucepan over low heat until hot. Thin with milk if necessary. Serve with rye crackers.

Michelle Krahenbuhl
Wisconsin Folklife Festival Participant
Cheesemaker
Monticello

4 oz. cream cheese

1/4 c. sour cream

4 oz. shaved corned beef, finely chopped

8 oz. shredded Emmenthaler cheese

1/4 c. drained and chopped sauerkraut

3 T. milk

rye crackers

Michelle Krahenbuhl
Wisconsin Folklife Festival Participant
Cheesemaker
Monticello

Fondue:

1 lb. Gouda cheese, cut into small cubes

3 T. flour

1 clove garlic, halved

1 can (12 ounces) beer OR 1-1/2 c. white
    wine

1 T. spicy brown mustard (optional)

Dippers:

unsliced rye bread (cut in 1-inch cubes
    and toasted)

blanched broccoli*

blanched cauliflower flowerets*

cooked small red potatoes

Gouda Fondue with Beer or Wine

Makes 8 servings

To make fondue, combine cubed cheese and flour in a mixing bowl; toss to mix. Rub bottom and sides of a heavy saucepan with cut surface of garlic halves. Discard garlic. Add beer or wine to saucepan. Heat over low heat just until warm. Gradually add small amounts of floured cheese, stirring constantly over low heat until all is melted. Stir in mustard, if desired. Transfer hot cheese mixture to a fondue pot, keep warm over fondue burner. Serve immediately with dippers. Swirl as you dip. If cheese mixture thickens while standing, stir in a little warm beer or wine. If you don't have a fondue pot, you can serve fondue in a casserole pot.

*Blanch broccoli and cauliflower flowerets in a small amount of boiling water for 3 minutes or until crisp and tender. Drain and rinse with cold water. Drain well.

White Girl Salsa

Makes approximately 50 ounces.

The real secret is to use fresh, locally grown, organic vegetables whenever possible. Listen to latino or central american music while preparing.

Chop garlic finely. With mortar and pestal, grind salt and garlic together, add oil and mix.

Put tomato paste and juices into large serving bowl. Add garlic mixture and stir. Add all remaining ingredients and mix well.

Serve with organic white, blue or yellow corn chips.

Try using apple cider vinegar to replace lemon and lime juice.

I made this recipe up by trying different salsas and creating one specifically to my taste. My friend, who is Puerto Rican, says its " the best salsa in the world - made by a white girl from Wisconsin!"
JoAnn Blohowiak
Graphic Designer of Home Cooked Culture:
Wisconsin Through Recipes
Green Bay

6 roma tomatoes, diced

4 cloves garlic

1/3 c fresh cilantro, chopped fine

juice from 1 medium lemon

juice from 1/2 medium lime

1/3 large red onion, chopped

1 c precooked black turtle beans or kidney beans

1/2 sm can tomato paste

1 green chili (to taste for hotness), chopped very fine

1 med green pepper, chopped

1 large ripe avacoado, chopped into big chunks

1 tsp salt

1 T olive or canola oil

1/8 tsp cayenne (to taste for hotness)

optional: 1 c fresh corn

Pancakes and Crepes

Wisconsin Through Recipes

ERRATA

On page 25, the ingredients for Beerwurst Soup are listed incorrectly. The correct ingredients for the soup are as follows:

1 c. celery, chopped
1 medium onion, chopped
2 T. butter or margarine
1 T. cornstarch
½ t. mustard, dry
¼ t. garlic powder
¼ t. oregano, dried

¼ t. basil, dried and crushed
¼ t. thyme, dried and crushed
(1) 12 oz. can beer
1 ¼ c. broth, condensed beef
4 slices French Bread
1 c. Mozzarella cheese, shredded
12 oz. Usinger's Beerwurst,
        thinly sliced and quartered

Palacinky (Slovak Crepes)

Sift flour (after measuring 1 cup). Combine sifted flour, sugar, and salt in blender. Add milk, eggs, and butter; blend to a smooth consistency. The batter should be thin. Pour a small amount of the batter into a heated, lightly greased skillet. When brown on the underside, flip over and brown on the other side. Remove from pan and place on a warm plate. Place about three large tablespoons cottage cheese in a line towards one side of the crepe. Sprinkle with 1/2 teaspoon sugar. Roll up and keep warm. Continue cooking and rolling crepes until all the batter is used. You may, if you wish, substitute jam for the cottage cheese, or use the jam with the cottage cheese instead of the sugar. Excellent.

Sidonka Wadina
Wisconsin Folklife Festival Participant
Wheat weaver
Lyons

Crepes:

1 c. flour

1 t. sugar

1/2 t. salt

1 1/2 c. milk

2 eggs

1 T. butter, melted

Filling:

2-3 c. small curd cottage cheese

additional sugar

Eleanor Bagstad
Wisconsin Folklife Festival Participant
Member of Norskedalen Trio
Westby

10 lbs. potatoes (Russet potatoes work best)

2 t. salt

2 T. vegetable oil

1/4 - 1 c. flour

Norwegian Lefse

Cook the potatoes the evening before until almost done. Add no salt. Drain well and mash with potato masher. Cool well. Store in refrigerator with a paper towel placed over bowl to collect moisture. Place aluminum foil over the paper towel.

In the morning, heat lefse grill to 400-500 F. Pass potatoes through a ricer. Add salt and oil. Mix well. Add flour. Knead and roll into a log. Cut into pieces (size is up to you). Roll out and bake on lefse grill until done, about 2-3 minutes.

Kropsua (Oven Pancakes)

Stir all ingredients together and put in a Pyrex pie pan. Bake at 400 F. 20 minutes. Serve warm with fruit, jelly or powdered sugar on top.

Irene Vuorenmaa
Wisconsin Folklife Festival Participant
Rag rug weaver
Hurley

4 c. milk

4 eggs

1/2 T. salt

1/2 c. sugar

1/4 c. melted butter

2 c. flour

Else Bigton: "This recipe is from my mother-in-law, Jean Odden. She's the best cook there is."
Phillip Odden/Else Bigton
Wisconsin Folklife Festival Participants
Norwegian wood carvers
Barronett

potatoes, preferably Russets: enough to make 3 cups cooked or riced potatoes

1/4 c. (4 tablespoons) melted butter

1 cup flour

1 T. sugar

1 t. salt

Norwegian Lefse

Cook potatoes with skins in boiling water. Drain and peel while still hot. Mash potatoes or pass them through a ricer, enough to make 3 cups. Stir melted butter into mashed potatoes while still warm, then thoroughly chill mixture in refrigerator.

When ready to cook lefse, add flour, sugar and salt to potatoes and mix well. Heat an electric frying pan to 400 F. or heat a lefse grill. Roll dough into balls (size is as desired) on floured surface. Use a grooved lefse pin (which will prevent bubbles from forming when baking) or a standard rolling pin to roll out balls: Cover rolling pin with cloth, then flour both the pin and the work surface. Roll out balls thinly. Bake in fry pan or lefse grill. Cool the lefse between layers of a folded cloth.

Annabelle Argand
Wisconsin Folklife Festival Participant
Jewish fabric art
Madison

Aunt Yetta's Potato Latkes

2 large raw white potatoes (about 1 lb.)

1 T. grated onion

2 eggs, unbeaten

2 T. uncooked oatmeal

2 T. flour

1 1/2 t. salt

pinch of pepper

salad oil

Makes 10-14 pancakes

The pancakes must be cooked immediately after preparing, as the mixture will darken if it stands.

Wash and peel raw potatoes. Working quickly, grate them on a fine grater. Drain off excess liquid well.

Quickly stir in onion, eggs, oatmeal, flour, salt, and pepper. Measure salad oil to a depth of 1/4 inch in skillet. Heat oil over medium heat. Drop mixture from a tablespoon into hot oil, spreading each cake with the back of a spoon until it is thin. Fry to a deep golden brown on both sides. Drain on paper towels.

Crepes

For batter, measure dry ingredients into a bowl. Stir in remaining batter ingredients. Beat until smooth. Lightly butter crepe pan or non-stick skillet and heat over medium flame. Pour small amount of batter (approximately 1/4 cup) into skillet. Immediately turn pan until batter covers the bottom. Cook until light brown. Turn crepe over and cook on the other side. Spread with jam, syrup or fresh fruit and roll up. Serve warm.

"This recipe was passed to me from my mom. She made these often for our family as a breakfast dish. Now crepes are the top request of my daughters when we visit grandma and grandpa."
Linda Ollerman
Wisconsin Folklife Festival Participant
Quilter from the Sew Happy Sewers
Ripon

Batter ingredients:

1 1/2 c. flour

1 T. sugar

1/2 t. baking powder

1/2 t. salt

2 c. milk

1/2 t. vanilla

2 T. butter or margarine, melted

grated peel of 1 orange (optional, but this is the extra touch that makes this recipe so tasty!)

2 eggs

Also:

additional butter for cooking

jam, syrup, or fresh fruit

"I got this recipe from my husband's grandmother. It was a recipe they made in her house when she was a child in Milwaukee. A simple food served for brunch or a light dinner on Sunday evenings. Absolutely delicious with warm applesauce!!"
Della Pleski
Sesquicentennial Folk Arts Exhibitor
Foxboro

Pancakes:

2 large baking potatoes

1 1/2 t. grated onion

2 T. flour

1/2 t. salt

2 T. milk

2 eggs, beaten

dash of pepper

dash of nutmeg

Also:

oil for frying

maple syrup or warm applesauce

Great Grandma's Potato Pancakes

about 1 dozen pancakes

Peel and soak potatoes in cold water for 2 hours. Drain potatoes and grate on a medium grater. You should get approximately 2 cups. Press grated potatoes through sieve until dry. Then place potatoes into medium mixing bowl. Add onion, flour, salt, milk, eggs, pepper and nutmeg. Mix well. Measure oil to 1/4-inch in skillet; heat over medium flame. Drop potato batter by tablespoonful. Spread mixture with back of spoon. Serve with syrup or warm applesauce.

Pancakes

Let oats stand in buttermilk while the other ingredients are measured. Beat all together until well blended. Cook pancakes on hot griddle.

*To substitute for buttermilk, add 1 tablespoon vinegar to 2 cups milk.

"The oatmeal and buttermilk in these pancakes make them delicious, and this is one of my favorite recipes from my grandma. She gave me a book of recipes from her sewing club, the "Shady Glen Sewing Club," which has been in existence since 1921. It's fun to have a cookbook with recipes from Grandma and her friends."
Kathy Oppegard
Wisconsin Folklife Festival Staff, Assistant Volunteer Coordinator
Madison

    1 1/2 c. oatmeal, raw

    2 c. buttermilk*

    2 beaten eggs

    1/2 c. flour

    1 t. salt

    1 t. baking soda

    1 t. sugar

Soups...
Wisconsin Through Recipes

Cherry Dumpling Soup

Makes 4 servings

To make soup, boil cherries, sugar and water in saucepan. To prepare dumplings, mix flour, baking powder and salt. Stir in egg and milk. Drop batter by spoonfuls over cherries. Keep covered and cook for 20 minutes over medium heat.

"A good way to use the famous cherries from Door County, Wisconsin."
Diana Schroeder
Wisconsin Folklife Festival Participant
Member, Clete Bellin Orchestra
Manitowoc

Soup:

1 quart cherries, pitted or unpitted

1/4 c. sugar

2 1/2 c. water (or add more water if you want it soupier)

Dumplings:

1 1/2 c. flour

1 t. baking powder

dash of salt

1 egg, beaten

1/4 c. milk

"A slow cooker will work real good. I was hunting in my duck skiff and had so much wild game, like rabbit and venison goose. That's how I made chili. The recipe is about 35 years old. I was hunting on the Bay of Green Bay when a DNR officer said, 'What do you do with all your wild game?' And I said, 'Make chili out of it,' as a joke. Then I came home and made it. It's good. Hunting party or just any time."
Patrick Farrell
Wisconsin Folklife Festival Participant
Skiff builder, decoy carver, canoe paddler
Green Bay

2 lbs. ground wild game or 1 lb. ground wild game and 1 lb. ground beef

1/2 cup chopped onions

2 T. vegetable oil

2 minced garlic cloves

2 T. chili powder

2 t. ground cumin

1 T. paprika

1 t. salt

white pepper to taste

black pepper to taste

1 can (28 oz.) tomatoes, with juices

1 can (8 oz.) tomato sauce

1 can (6 oz.) tomato paste

1 can (15 oz.) kidney beans

1 can (15 oz.) pinto beans

Wild Game Chili

Cook wild game beef and onions in oil until brown. Add garlic, all the seasonings, tomatoes, tomato sauce, tomato paste and 1 cup water. Cover. Bring to a boil over high heat. Reduce heat and simmer 1 hour or longer. Add beans and heat through. Adjust seasonings to taste. Best when prepared a day ahead and reheated before serving.

Wild Rice Soup

Put all ingredients except cheese in crock pot. Cover with water. Cook on high 1 hour. Reduce heat to low and cook at least 2 more hours. Stir in cheese 1/2 hour before serving time.

"I made up this recipe. It is 5-6 years old and is good for cold, blustery days in Wisconsin and the annual Christmas pheasant hunt. This soup is very good with homemade bread."
Dennis O'Donnell
Wisconsin Folklife Festival Participant
Welder and Dairy Farmer
Frederic

2 c. cooked wild rice

1 c. frozen corn

1 c. frozen peas

1 c. chopped frozen broccoli

1 c. chopped frozen cauliflower

1 c. sliced frozen carrots

1/2 lb. bacon, cooked and diced

2 t. chicken bouillon

1 lb. Velveeta cheese, cubed

Betty Christenson
Wisconsin Folklife Festival Participant
Ukrainian egg decorator
Suring

6-8 young beets, with stalk and leaves

5 c. warm water

1 medium onion, chopped

1/2 c. broad or fresh green beans,
    chopped

1/2 c. fresh peas

1/2 c. diced potatoes

1/4 c. chopped fresh dill

1 few fresh garlic leaves, chopped

2 t. salt

2 T. lemon juice or vinegar

3 T. flour

1/2 c. water

1 c. cream or milk

Creamed Spring Borsch (Beet Soup)

Makes 6-8 servings

Wash beets thoroughly but do not peel. Rinse stalks and leaves. Set leaves aside. Dice beets and stalks. Combine in a large pot: chopped beets, chopped stalks, warm water, onion, beans, peas, potatoes, dill, garlic leaves, salt and lemon juice. Bring to simmer and cook until tender. Do not overcook vegetables. Add the diced beet leaves last. When vegetables are almost done, mix flour with 1/2 c. water. Stir flour mixture into soup. Cook 5 minutes. Add cream or milk and serve.

Denzin Manke Cherry Soup

To make soup: Boil water with 1 or 11/2 cups sugar. Add cherries and cook to soften. Check sweetness and add more sugar if necessary. Bring to a steady boil.

Meanwhile, mix dumpling ingredients in a bowl. It will look like cake batter. Dribble or slowly pour dumpling mixture into boiling soup. Continue cooking while dribbling in the dumpling mixture. Remove from heat. Can be eaten warm or cold.

"Once a year, at the peak of the cherry season, my father would make cherry soup. As a child, I remember pitting endless pails of cherries with a hairpin in preparation of cherry soup. My dad got the recipe from his mother who got it from her mother, who brought it with her to Milwaukee from Pommerania, Germany in the 1860's. My father's recipe was passed down from word of mouth and was not written down. This is a traditional Pommeranian recipe."
Chris Manke
Wisconsin Arts Board Staff, Percent for Arts Coordinator
Madison

Soup:

4-7 c. water

1- 2 3/4 c. sugar

3-6 c. pitted sour cherries

Dumplings:

1-2 eggs, beaten

1/2 - 1 t. baking powder

4-8 T. flour

1/4 - 1/2 c. milk

pinch of salt

Rita Horvath
Wisconsin Folklife Festival Staff, Supply Coordinator
Madison

Soup:

1 medium yellow onion, cubed

oil for sautéing

3 t. paprika

2 c. cubed beef

salt

1 sliced parsnip

3 medium carrots, sliced

small bunch of celery leaves, chopped

2 large potatoes, cubed

Dumplings:

1 c. flour

1 egg

salt

Hungarian Goulash Soup

Sauté onion in large soup pot with the oil. Add paprika and mix immediately. Quickly add cubed beef to the pot and mix. Add 1/2 gallon water (or to cover ingredients) and salt to taste.

Let soup simmer while you make dumplings: Put flour in medium mixing bowl. Add one whole egg and salt to taste. Mix the ingredients with your hands until the mixture is stiff. Add more flour if needed. Set aside.

When meat is half cooked, add parsnip, carrot and celery leaves. Cook for 5-7 minutes. Then add potatoes and cook thoroughly. With soup boiling, pinch off a thumb-sized amount of dumpling mixture into soup pot. Repeat until all the dumpling mixture has been used. When dumplings float to stop of soup, cook 1-2 minutes longer and serve.

Variation: Bean Goulash Soup

Proceed as directed in Hungarian goulash soup recipe. Substitute a 12 ounce can of beans (any kind) for the 2 large potatoes. Prepare as directed. Serve with Pogacsa (biscuits, see recipe in Breads, Rolls and Muffins p.76).

Beerwurst Soup

Makes 4 servings

In large skillet cook celery and onion in butter or margarine until tender but not brown. Blend in cornstarch, dry mustard, garlic powder, oregano, basil and thyme; add beer and beef broth. Cook and stir until thickened and bubbly. Cover and simmer over low heat for 30 minutes, stirring occasionally.

Meanwhile, arrange bread slices on a baking sheet; sprinkle cheese on top. Broil 3 inches from heat for 3 minutes or until cheese is melted and lightly browned. Add Beerwurst to soup; simmer 2-3 minutes to heat thoroughly. Top soup with hot bread slices.

Debra Usinger
(Recipe from Usinger's Recipe Collections
Wisconsin Folklife Festival Participant
Sausage making and cookery
Milwaukee

2 quarts white flint (Indian) dry corn

3 heaping T. baking soda

1 can (15 oz.) red, pinto or kidney beans, drained

1 lb. salt pork or other pork meat, simmered in water until tender

Indian Corn Soup

In a large kettle, simmer 1 gallon of water and sorted, clean corn with baking soda for 3 hours. Corn hulls should be slippery to the touch. Watch corn so it does not get brown in color. Rinse corn 5-6 times. Simmer for 1 more hour. Drain and rinse once. Corn is now ready for soup.

Cut up the cooked meat. Add meat and beans to corn. Add enough water (you can also use broth from meat) to cover. Simmer 1-2 hours. If you cook the meat the day before and refrigerate, you can remove the fat before using the broth.

Paul "Sugar Bear" Smith
Wisconsin Folklife Festival Participant
Native American agriculturist
Oneida

2 quarts white flint (Indian) dry corn

3 heaping T. baking soda

1 can (15 oz.) red, pinto or kidney beans, drained

1 lb. salt pork or other pork meat, simmered in water until tender

Michelle Krahenbuhl
Wisconsin Folklife Festival Participant
Cheesemaker
Monticello

3 T. butter

1 medium onion, chopped

4 green onions, chopped

1 clove garlic, pressed

3 medium carrots, peeled and sliced

2 medium potatoes, peeled and cubed

1/3 c. all-purpose flour

2 T. cornstarch

3 c. chicken broth

1/2 c. sherry

1/4 c. whipping cream

1/2 t. garlic powder

1/2 t. onion powder

dash of nutmeg

1/2 t. salt

1/2 t. white pepper

2 cups cubed Gouda cheese

Sherried Cheese Soup

Makes 4 servings

Heat butter in 3-quart saucepan; add onion, green onions and garlic and cook until soft, stirring occasionally. Stir in carrots and potatoes; cook over medium heat for 10 minutes, stirring occasionally. Add flour and cornstarch, stirring constantly. Add broth and sherry and simmer for several minutes, until slightly thickened. Reduce heat to low; add cream and seasonings. Stirring constantly, add cheese cubes a little at a time, allowing each addition of cheese to melt before adding more. Do not allow soup to boil as you add the cheese. Serve hot.

Chicken Bouyon (or Booyah)

Makes 10-12 servings

To cook chicken: Place roasting/stewing hen in a 12-quart kettle. Add chopped onion, salt and pepper. Add 4 quarts of water, cover, and bring to a boil.

Reduce heat and simmer slowly until chicken is tender and flesh falls from the bones. Remove the chicken to a large stainless steel bowl; set aside to cool. Remove flesh from bones. Strain chicken stock and cool. Remove fat from surface.

To make soup: Return cooled chicken stock and 4 quarts cold water to a 12-quart kettle; bring to a boil. Reduce heat, add carrots, celery and onion, salt and pepper. Simmer until vegetables are tender. Add egg noodles (or potatoes) and simmer for 5 minutes. Add the boned chicken meat and heat through. If you include the tomato soup and canned peas in the recipe, add those ingredients along with the boned chicken meat at the very end. Dried navy beans, corn, shredded green cabbage, ox tail bones, beef bones and pork bones are just some of the additional ingredients added to the

"(Here) is my recipe for Chicken Bouyon. It's actually my sister, Ruth Frisque's, recipe which I borrowed, since I do not make my bouyon from a recipe. I always make it from scratch, with a pinch of this and a pinch of that to taste. However, with the exception of the potatoes, tomato soup and peas, the ingredients are identical. I always use noodles in my recipe, as did most of our great, great grand-parents that came from the Walloon (Southern) part of Belgium. They did not have the luxury of going to a grocery store to buy canned tomato soup or canned peas, and always made homemade egg noodles, which were a staple part of the bouyon. This was a soup-type dish that was made only for very special occasions and holidays and for the Kermiss (Karmesse). It was a thick hearty dish that literally "stuck to your ribs."

Godefroid de Bouillon, born in 1061, was a noble-man of the House of Bouillon in Wallonia, in what is today southern Belgium. He led the First Crusade from 1096-1099, and was crowned the first king of Jerusalem in 1099. He died in 1100. Although there is no historical verification, perhaps the bouyon we make to this very day had its origin in the kitchen at the castle of Bouillon and was made to nourish the crusading knights and nobles of the realm. Whatever the case, it is unique to the Walloon Belgians and was only made by them and their descendants. Now, with its many additions and variations, it has been adopted by and is made by all kinds of nationalities in Northeast Wisconsin. I hope you enjoy making the recipe someday. Bon appetit!"

basic recipe by today's cooks to enhance the flavor and context of the bouyon. Beef bouyon can also be made by substituting beef (brisket or other less expensive cuts along with beef bones for flavor) for the chicken in this recipe. Serve with your favorite crackers or crisp French bread.

*If you include noodles in the recipe, it is customary to eliminate the potatoes. If you add the potatoes, then you eliminate the noodles. While the amount of noodles given for the recipe is from 4-6 cups, the actual amount can be adjusted to your individual preference. If you like more, add more; if you like less, add less. I personally like a lot of noodles in my recipe, so the amount I use varies.

Clete Bellin
Wisconsin Folklife Festival Participant
Clete Bellin Orchestra
Forestville

Chicken:

1 large roasting/stewing hen, about 6 lbs.

1 small onion, chopped

salt and pepper to taste

4 quarts cold water

Soup:

4 quarts cold water

1 bunch carrots, peeled and sliced 1/4-inch thick

1 large bunch celery, including leaves, diced

1 large onion, diced

salt and pepper to taste

4-6 c. egg noodles* (homemade if possible) OR 6 large potatoes, diced

2 cans (each 16 oz.) tomato soup (optional)

1 can (16 oz.) peas, with juice (optional)

Side Dishe s . . .

Wisconsin Through Recipes

"We use it quite often just because we like it. Can be made as spicy as you like...I cannot be more specific on the vinegar and sugar because my mother never had a recipe. This is the way she taught us."
Norma Belliveau
Wisconsin Folklife Festival Participant
Wreath maker and Tree Farmer
Tomahawk

    butter for sautéing

    1 large head of cabbage, sliced

    1 large onion, chopped

    vinegar and sugar to taste

    1/2 t. garlic salt or powder

    salt and pepper to taste

Sweet Sour Cabbage

Heat butter in large skillet. Add cabbage and onion; saute until tender. Add vinegar and sugar to taste. Season with garlic salt or powder, salt and pepper. The cabbage will cook down considerably after the vinegar is added. Let stand a few minutes before serving.

Dandelion Greens

Using a paring knife, cut greens by the clump or bunch (cut from under ground). Shake foreign materials such as dried leaves, weeds or bugs, from greens. Wash the greens several times. Place clean greens in pan with 1 cup of water. Bring to a hard boil. Stir with a fork. Drain water off and put in a little water, salt and pepper and vinegar. Cover and cook for 15 minutes until greens are tender. Add bacon pieces, chopped ham or butter for flavor.

"My parents and my husband's parents have made this dish since early 1900's. They are rich in iron and vitamins."
Inez Robertson
Wisconsin Sesquicentennial Folk Arts Exhibitor
Sheldon

fresh young dandelion greens

salt and pepper

vinegar or sweet pickle vinegar

fried bacon or chopped ham or butter

"My mother got this recipe from her neighbor Norma Cashin. Norma Cashin won a first prize recipe at the Wisconsin State Fair in the 1940's. The recipe is very old, probably originating in 1920-1930's. I have sent the original recipe. My mother modified the recipe to reflect contemporary canning practices. Rather than bake the jars of dill pickles in an oven, she kept the brine boiling and sealed the jars often putting boiling brine in the pickle jars. My mother made these pickles every August and as children, we eagerly awaited the end of the two-month curing time to eat the pickles."
Chris Manke
Wisconsin Arts Board Staff, Percent for Arts Coordinator
Madison

Pickles:

pickling cucumbers

dill weed fronds

1/2 c. mustard seed

1 head garlic cloves, sliced

pea-size pieces of alum

Brine:

3 c. water

1 c. vinegar

1/4 c. salt

Norma Cashin's Dill Pickles

(Note: This recipe assumes the cook has some canning experience. If you have never canned before, be sure to follow general canning instructions from a reliable source)

Prepare quart jars, lids, and screw bands for canning. Scrub cucumbers. Place dill frond in bottom of each jar. Fill jar with clean cucumbers. (Place cucumbers vertically in jars.) Place second dill frond on top of cucumbers in each jar. Add 1/2 teaspoon mustard seed to each jar along with sliced garlic cloves as desired. Place pea size hunk of alum in each jar. Boil brine ingredients. Fill jars with brine. Seal with prepared lids. Place jars of pickles in baking pan and bake 20 minutes in 300 F. oven. Remove from oven to cool. Check seals. Let pickles sit 2 months before opening.

Sichuan Noodles

Bring large pot of water to boil. Add noodles; cook according to package directions. Drain and run noodles under cold water until chilled. Drain well. Sprinkle with teaspoon of sesame oil and toss to coat. Set aside.

Mix together sauce ingredients and pour over noodles. Mix thoroughly. Let stand 1/2 hour before serving in order to blend flavors. Garnish with diced green onions and fresh cilantro.

"A friend gave me the recipe in the early 1960's. I have made it for many, many pot luck events and it is always a big hit. For many years, I refused to give out the recipe as it was my one "secret" recipe. I no longer make the recipe as I have developed allergies to peanuts, a main ingredient. Here is the original recipe, although I never followed the recipe but improvised freely.
Chris Manke
Wisconsin Arts Board Staff, Percent for Arts Coordinator
Madison

Noodles:

12 oz. Asian egg noodles or fine spaghetti

1 t. dark sesame oil

Sauce:

1 t. to 1 T. garlic chili paste (available in Asian food stores)

3 T. light soy sauce

3 T. red wine vinegar

3 t. sugar, or to taste

3 t. salt, or to taste

1/4 - 1/2 c. peanut oil

1 T. dark sesame oil

Garnish:

chopped green onions

chopped fresh cilantro

"These dumplings were made by my grandmother whenever the plums were in season or available. My grandmother was born near the Hungarian border in Austria in 1885, and they were made by her mother and probably her grandmother also. When fresh, they were served as a dessert or a side dish. They were sliced and eaten cold as a snack or sliced and lightly fried for lunch or breakfast. My memory of these dumplings goes back to the 1930's. It was a hardy, filling "Depression" dish and also filled a need for a sweet treat since sweet desserts were not readily available.

This same dough may be rolled and cut off the edge of a board into the boiling water and makes wonderful little dumplings which my grandmother then added to cabbage which was cooked in a frying pan with caraway until nice and brown. She would let the steam cook away and fry the cabbage and dumplings together until it was scrumptious. For the dumplings she would make two smaller rolls rather than the larger one for the plum dumplings."

Elfrieda Haese
Wisconsin Folklife Festival Participant
Haese and Schlei, Austrian Music
Colgate

2 c. mashed potatoes (not warm)	8-10 Italian plums
1 egg	1/2 c. sugar
pinch of salt	1 t. cinnamon
1 1/2 - 2 c. flour	1/2 c. (1 stick) butter
	1 c. bread crumbs

Plum Dumplings

Place potatoes in a mixing bowl. Add egg and salt. Add about a cup of flour and work mixture into a smooth dough. It will be sticky at first, but keep adding flour until it reaches the right consistency. The dough should be sturdy (but not stiff) enough to roll around a plum. It helps to use a floured board and to keep your hands floured. I usually work my dough into a long fat roll and break off a chunk, flattening it with my hand for each dumpling; but dough can be rolled and cut into squares. Set dough aside.

Remove pits from plums. Mix with sugar and cinnamon. Roll a chunk of dough around each plum and pinch together to seal. You should be rolling the dough into a ball with your hand, and patting it at the same time.

Bring salted water to boil in a large pot. Drop dumplings in one by one. Boil for about 10 minutes after they rise to the top. Meanwhile, melt butter in a large frying pan, add breadcrumbs and brown well. Drain dumplings and roll them in the crumbs.

Corn Mush

Brown corn in oven at 300 F. until lightly brown. Grind up coarsely in food processor, blender, coffee grinder, or old-fashioned mortar and pestle. Mix 1 cup of the ground corn with remaining ingredients. (Reserve remaining ground corn for next time you make the cereal.) Simmer 15 minutes. Let sit 5 minutes before eating.

"We also add blueberries and strawberries to this cereal. Many Indians today have diabetes. The blueberry is a blood sugar regulator and the strawberries come all the way from our creation story. They're a medicine for us. The blueberries, strawberries and maple syrup are all ingredients that are a part of our culture."
Paul "Sugar Bear" Smith
Wisconsin Folklife Festival Participant
Native American agriculturist
Oneida

1 quart white flint (Indian) dry corn

3 c. boiling water

1 T. oil

3 T. maple syrup

"I'm submitting a recipe for Busia's Potato Cake. The smell always brought joy to my heart and with syrup poured over the top, you can't beat it."
Emma Czarapata
Wisconsin Folklife Festival Volunteer
Madison

8 large, raw potatoes, grated

1 large onion, grated

2 eggs

2 T. flour

4-6 slices bacon cut into pieces (ham may be used)

2 t. salt

pepper

Busia's Potato Cake

Place ingredients in bowl and mix well. Pour into a well-greased baking or oven-proof frying pan and bake in moderate oven (350 F.) until nice and brown.

Main Dishes...

Wisconsin Through Recipes

Prime Rib Wild Mallard Canvas Back

(or other large duck)

Harold Hettrick
Wisconsin Folklife Festival Participant
Duck hunter
Madison

Pick and clean duck thoroughly. Dry with paper towels. Rub Pleasoning salt, pepper, and sage to taste over entire duck.

Place cast iron Dutch pan in oven and heat at 550 F. 20 minutes. Place ducks breast side up in hot cast iron pan. If you like the ducks well done, put a pre-heated cover over pan. Close oven door. Cook ducks 22 minutes, then turn off oven and let ducks sit in heated oven another 22 minutes.

1 large wild duck per person

Pleasoning salt

pepper

ground sage

large, deep cast iron Dutch oven

"My father is from Michoacan. I was born and raised (in the United States) but I spent my youth going back and forth. My mother is from Zacatecas; this recipe is hers and my aunts'. I talked to each one of my aunts separately; (it's) a combination of many recipes. Some people use a microwave to cook tamales or use other (time-saving methods). My ancestors would probably roll over in their graves! I do it mostly the old way."
Rosa Chavez
Wisconsin Folklife Festival Participant
Day of the Dead Altar maker
Franklin

3-4 lb. bone-in pork roast

1-2 t. salt

5-6 cloves garlic, divided

5 large dried ancho peppers

4-6 large tomatillos

Corn husks:

4-5 dozen dried corn husks (try to get large ones)

Dough:

2 1/4 lbs. masa harina (corn masa mix)

1 t. baking powder

1 1/2 t. salt

1 c. lard (homemade is better than commercial lard)

broth from the cooked pork roast

Tamales

Makes 2-3 dozen tamales

Filling:

To make filling: Remove visible fat from pork roast. Place roast in pot and cover with water. Add salt and 2-3 cloves of the garlic. Bring to simmer; cook over low heat until meat is very tender. (Reserve the broth for the dough). Cool meat and broth. Chop roast into small pieces. Strain broth.

Seed, de-vein and remove stems from anchos. Put them in microwaveable bowl. Add enough water to cover peppers. Microwave 2-3 minutes. Let soak until anchos are soft. Meanwhile, remove papery outer skin from tomatillos; cut open and remove seeds. Put softened ancho peppers, tomatillos and remaining garlic in blender. Add a little water from the peppers. Blend until smooth. Combine this red sauce with the diced pork in a small saucepan. Cover and simmer over low flame until the sauce has thickened. Cool.

To prepare corn husks: Soak husks in hot water 20-30 minutes. Remove any "hair." Drain on paper towels. (You'll use the wider, larger husks for the tamales.)

To make dough: Combine masa harina, baking powder and salt in bowl. Beat lard in separate bowl with an electric mixer until light and fluffy. Slowly add dry ingredients to the lard. Add pork broth a little at a time and knead dough. Dough should be smooth and soft, and neither dry nor watery.

To prepare cooking pot(s): Use smaller corn husks to line the bottom of a steam basket or perforated pot. Fill a larger pot with a few inches of water (enough to come up to where the steam basket will fit inside of the larger pot). Place pot with water in it over high flame; bring to boil; lower heat to low. (Some people put a coin into the water because it will make a noise as the tamales steam, indicating if the water is boiling or low.) You may also prepare the pot after all the tamales have been filled.

To fill and cook tamales: Place corn husk-lined steam basket or perforated pot in larger pot. Take a large corn husk and open it with the point up. Take a table-spoon of dough and mold it into the shape of a ball. Place the ball of dough in the middle of the lower part of the husk. Make an indentation in the dough and add a heaping teaspoon of cooled filling. Fold the right side over the dough and filling. Do the same with the left side. The right and left sides should overlap. Fold the filled corn husk in half, with the open side up. Repeat with corn husks and filling. Place filled tamales upright, open side up, in corn husk-lined steam basket. Tamales should be close together but not tight. After the pot is filled, cover with remaining corn husks and a damp dish towel. Cover pot tightly with a lid. Steam tamales over medium-low heat about 1 hour or until dough puffs easily from the husk. (If the pot is covered tightly, the water won't boil away; but to be sure, check occasionally and add more boiling water if necessary). Serve tamales warm.

Main dishes

Tomato Soup:

1 1/2 lbs. tomatoes (about 3 large tomatoes), peeled and seeded

3-5 cups water and 1 chicken bouillon cube OR 3-5 cups chicken stock

3/4 medium onion, chopped

1 clove garlic

salt to taste

Peppers:

6 poblano peppers (chiles poblanos)

Frying oil:

canola or safflower oil

Egg batter:

6 eggs, separated and brought to room temperature

pinch of salt

pinch of flour

Filling(select one):

1. Chihuahua or Oaxaca cheese (Muenster, Monterey Jack or Brick cheese will also do), cut into strips;

OR

2. Potato filling made from 2 medium potatoes, cooked and mashed, then combined with a little queso fresco or Parmesan, a little milk, and salt to taste;

OR

3. 1 can tuna fish in water or oil, well-drained

Chiles Rellenos (Stuffed Peppers) with Tomato Soup

To make soup:

Place tomatoes in medium-sized pot. Add just enough water (and bouillon cube) or chicken stock to cover. Bring to boil. Remove tomatoes with slotted spoon; peel and seed them. Place tomatoes, cooking liquid and remaining sauce ingredients except salt in blender. Blend until liquefied. Strain out any remaining seeds, if desired. Place mixture in pot; cover and simmer over low flame until lightly thickened and smooth, 40-50 minutes. Add salt to taste. Keep warm.

To prepare peppers:

Roast peppers over direct flame until they blister. Turn frequently as to not overcook peppers. Put in plastic bag and tie or cover with damp kitchen towel. Leave for 15-20 minutes. Put on plastic gloves to protect hands. Peel peppers. Carefully make a slit in each pepper and remove seeds and vein. Be sure to keep stem and top intact. If peppers have a strong, spicy odor they are probably hot. You may choose to soak them in a light vinegar and water solution for 20-30 minutes. Pat peppers dry. The egg mixture will adhere best to well-dried peppers. Fill peppers with one of the fillings: strips of cheese, potato filling, or tuna. Close the slit on each pepper and secure with a toothpick. Set stuffed peppers aside on paper towel.

To make egg batter and cook peppers:

Heat a little canola or safflower oil in a non-stick pan over medium flame; keep hot, but don't let it burn. Meanwhile, beat room-temperature egg whites in clean mixer on high speed. (It is very important that egg whites be at room temperature. This allows them to have more volume). When egg whites form peaks, add the yolks one by one, and continue beating. Add salt and flour. This flour helps the egg to adhere to the peppers. Quickly dip peppers in egg mixture and place peppers in pan. (Traditionally, peppers were deep fried, but I prefer a lighter version.) Cover pan. When egg is golden brown on one side, turn peppers over, and cover pan again. If there is leftover egg, form patties with spoon and cook the same way or coat cooked vegetables, and lightly fry them. (Cauliflower is a favorite.) Drain peppers and cooked egg or vegetables on paper towels.

To serve:

Ladle warm soup into shallow soup bowls. Place a pepper in each bowl and enjoy!

"There is no warmer place than the kitchen and I don't mean temperature. My husband says, 'People who love to cook are happy people.'"
Rosa Chavez
Wisconsin Folklife Festival Participant
Day of the Dead Altar maker
Franklin

Dorothy Hodgson
Wisconsin Folklife Festival Participant
Pasty Maker
Shullsburg

Filling:

1 1/2 lbs. potatoes

1 medium onion, chopped

1 lb. round steak, cubed

salt and pepper

Crust:

2 c. flour

1/2 lb. lard

just enough water to make dough soft

2 T. butter

Pasties
(Meat and Potato-Filled Turnovers)

Makes 2 large servings

Heat oven to 350 F. To make the filling, mix potatoes, chopped onions and steak. Season with salt and pepper to taste. Mix flour and lard to make the pie crust dough. Add just enough water to make dough soft. Roll out dough into two 8-inch circles. In the center of each circle, put half the filling. Put a tablespoon of butter over each mound of filling. Fold the circle over and crimp the edges. Place pasties on a cookie sheet and make a slit in the top of each. Bake 1-2 hours.

"I have been canning venison for over 25 years now. It is an excellent way to use up tougher meats, odd cuts, etc. that might otherwise be used in sausage or hamburger. It is also an excellent way to use (frozen) meat from the previous season when fresh venison has been taken. This recipe is excellent for hot beef sandwiches over potatoes, or can be added to hot dishes and soups. It is great for a quiche meal on hunting, fishing, or camping trips. For certain, it is much easier to store than trying to keep meat in a freezer for any length of time."
Mert Cowley
Wisconsin Folklife Festival Participant
Deer Camp Demonstrator and "Jack Pine Poet"
Chetek

For each quart::

venison, cut into 1 to 1 1/2-inch cubes

2 beef bouillon cubes

1 garlic clove

1 heaping t. onion soup

1/2 t. salt

Cowley's Canned Venison

The following are some important general instructions for canning from the Kerr company:

Raw Pack Method: Examine jars. They must be free of nicks, cracks, sharp edges, etc. Wash jars in hot, soapy water. If food is to be processed for less than 10 minutes, jars must be pre-sterilized in boiling water for 10 minutes. Add 1 minute for each 1000 feet of altitude. Scald (pour boiling water over) Kerr lids and keep in water at least 3 minutes or until used. DO NOT boil lids.

Select fresh, firm (not over-ripe) foods. Prepare according to recipe. Pack all foods loosely; fill all vegetables, grapes, meats and fish to within one inch of jar top. fill all other foods within 1/2 inch of jar top.

Use Raw Pack for Meats: Add no liquid. Natural meat juices will form. Before filling jars, wipe top of jars clean. Fill. Place scalded Kerr lid on jar with sealing composition next to the glass. Screw bands FIRMLY TIGHT. Do not use screw bands that are rusty or have top edge pried up. They will cause sealing failures.

To process: Place jars on rack in pressure canner

and process required length of time. Put on full heat until steam comes out vent hole in continuous stream. Vent for 10 minutes before placing pressure control over vent. When control vibrates rapidly, reduce heat so control vibrates 3-4 times per minute. Begin timing at first rapid vibration of pressure control. Allow pressure canner to cool as directed in recipe before removing jars. When jars are cool, TEST FOR SEAL: Press center of lid if it is down and will not move, jar is sealed. Refrigerate any jars that have not sealed.

When jars are cool and sealed, remove screw bands. Wash and dry bands. Bands are unnecessary once jars are sealed. Wash jars of food in soapy water before storing.

To prepare Cowley's Canned Venison:

Tightly pack cubed venison to within 1 inch of neck of quart jars. Get all the air out you can. Top each quart with 2 beef bouillon cubes, 1 garlic clove, 1 heaping teaspoon dried onion soup mix, and 1/2 teaspoon salt. Pressure cook 90 minutes at 10 pounds, following preceding instructions. Allow 1 hour for canner to cool down before attempting to remove jars. Any canned meats should be heated to a boil for several minutes prior to serving to avoid any possible problems.

Marlene Dombrowski
wife of Norm Dombrowski,
Wisconsin Folklife Participant
member of the Happy Notes Orchestra
Stevens Point

1 whole head of cabbage (about 4
  pounds)

salted, boiling water

1 onion, chopped

2 T. oil

1 1/2 lbs. ground beef

1/2 lb. freshly ground pork

1 1/2 c. cooked rice

1 t. salt

1/4 t. pepper

2 cans (about 10 oz. each) condensed
  tomato soup

2 1/2 c. water

Golabki (Stuffed Cabbage Rolls)

Makes about 15 servings

Remove core from cabbage. Place whole head in a large kettle filled with boiling salted water. Cover; cook for 3 minutes or until softened enough to pull off individual leaves. Repeat to remove all large leaves (about 30). Cut thick center stem from each leaf. Chop the remaining cabbage.

Sauté onion in oil. Add meats, rice, salt and pepper. Mix thoroughly.

Place a heaping teaspoon of meat mixture on a cabbage leaf. Tuck sides over filling while rolling leaf around filling. Secure with wooden pick. Repeat with remaining cabbage leaves and filling.

Place half the chopped cabbage on the bottom of a large Dutch oven. Fill with layers of the cabbage rolls. Cover with the remaining chopped cabbage.

Combine tomato soup with water; mix until smooth. Pour over cabbage rolls. Cover and bring to boiling. Reduce heat and simmer 1 1/2 hours. Serve cabbage rolls with the sauce.

Stuffed Pumpkins

Heat oven to 375 F. brown venison with onions in hot skillet. Drain off fat. Add water chestnuts, cream of mushroom soup, mushrooms, wild rice and soy sauce. Mix well. Cut top of pumpkin to make a lid. Scoop out pumpkin pulp and seeds. Wash out completely. Sprinkle inside of pumpkin with salt and pepper to taste. Spoon rice mixture into pumpkin shell. Bake one hour or until pumpkin is tender (fork should insert easily, but pumpkin should not be mushy).

" This dish can be prepared for Halloween or for a feast. If you want, you can paint your face on the pumpkin with a permanent marker before baking."
Elizabeth Lacapa
Wisconsin Folklife Festival Participant
Wild Rice Camp
Hayward

1 lb. venison hamburger

1 c. chopped onions

1 can (8 oz., including liquid) sliced water chestnuts, drained

2 cans (each 10.5 oz.) cream of mushroom soup

2 small cans (each 6.5 oz., including liquid) mushrooms, drained

2 c. cooked wild rice

2 T soy sauce

1 small pumpkin

"This is a dish to serve when you don't feel like preparing a huge meal. It's very filling, not to say rich, too!"
Jean Giese
Wisconsin Folklife Festival Participant
Rosemaling demonstrator
De Soto

Batter:

6 T. butter

1 c. flour

3 c. sweet milk

pinch salt Topping:

sugar

butter

cinnamon

Floisgrod

To make batter: Melt butter in saucepan over low heat. Add flour and salt and stir until well blended. Add the milk gradually. Stir continuously until smooth. Cook until thick, then serve hot topped with sugar, butter and cinnamon.

Geschnetzletz

Makes 4 servings

Trim fat off meat. Cut against grain into strips. Heat butter in large skillet over medium flame. Add onion and mushrooms. Cook 3 minutes or until golden brown. Add veal. Cook for 3 minutes, stirring constantly. Sprinkle flour over veal. Stir in pepper, paprika and salt. Add wine, beef stock and sour cream. Cook over low heat, stirring constantly, until mixture comes to just below boiling point and thickens. Sprinkle with parsley. Serve over noodles.

"This recipe shows a typical way the people of Glarus, Switzerland used veal. Many Glarners used veal in some manner. Being of totally Swiss ancestors, I like to use this recipe to carry on the Swiss traditions within my own family."
Elda Schiesser
Wisconsin Folklife Festival Participant
Swiss paper cutting
New Glarus

1/2 lb. veal

4 T. butter

3 T. chopped onion

2 cups sliced fresh mushrooms

1/4 c. flour

1/4 t. pepper

1/4 t. paprika

1/4 t. salt

1 c. dry white wine

1 c. beef stock

3/4 c. sour cream

2 T. chopped parsley

cooked noodles

2 lbs. veal, ground

1/2 lb. pork, ground

4 eggs

1 c. light cream

1/4 c. milk

1/4 c. finely chopped onion

1/4 t. nutmeg

1 t. salt

1/4 t. pepper

6 slices toasted bread, finely crumbled

6 T. butter or margarine

1 T. flour

1 c. milk or water

Chalber Balleli (Veal Balls)

6 servings

Mix veal and pork with eggs and cream that has been diluted with milk. Stir in onion. Season with nutmeg, salt and pepper. Crumble toast to make fine crumbs and mix in thoroughly. Form meat mixture into balls about the size of an egg. Heat oven to 350 F. Heat butter in skillet. Add veal balls and brown on all sides. Transfer veal balls and any fat from the pan into casserole dish. Cover and bake 30 minutes. Uncover and continue to bake until veal balls brown, approximately 10 minutes. Transfer veal balls to serving platter and set aside in warm place. Combine flour and juice from bottom of casserole in a skillet and brown slightly. Add milk or water and stir until lightly thickened. Pour gravy over veal balls or serve in a separate bowl.

Friday Fish Fry

Prepare Mies mixture according to instructions on the box. Set aside. Wash and prepare fish. Make sure fish is no more than 3/4 inch thick. Dry fish. Roll fish in "Mies" mix. Let fish sit on waxed paper for 10 minutes.

Meanwhile, pour canola oil into deep frying pan. Place strips of bacon in pan. When oil is 375 F., place the battered fish into frying pan. Fry fish one at a time, or a few at a time if they are small. Fish is cooked when it floats to the top and flakes in the middle. Drain fish on paper towels and serve. Enjoy!

"I use native Wisconsin fish in my fish fry: yellow perch, crappies, bluegills, small mouth bass, walleye, northern pike. I use Mies brand; it's a batter mix. I use it dry. I serve fish fry with fried potatoes: I bake potatoes, slice em 1/4-inch thick, fry em in a cast iron skillet with canola oil. When I flip em, I add diced onion, and sometimes a little green pepper. Plus you've gotta have cole slaw and rye bread. Beer is a given...gotta have it."
Harold Hettrick
Wisconsin Folklife Festival Participant
Duck hunter
Madison

"Mies" brand batter mix

your choice of fish fillets

waxed paper

canola oil

2 strips bacon or 1 T. bacon fat

Marlene Dombrowski
Wife of Norm Dombrowski, Wisconsin Folklife Festival
Participant
Member of the Happy Notes Band
Stevens Point

2 lbs. steak, round

1 c. bread crumbs

1 onion, grated

1 egg, beaten

8 T. butter, melted

1 T. parsley, chopped

2 c. water

salt and pepper to taste

Beef Roll-ups

Cut steak into thin pieces, about 4 1/2 x 2 inches. Score. Sprinkle with salt and pepper. Combine bread crumbs, egg, onion, 4 tablespoons melted butter, salt and pepper. Spread the dressing on each piece of meat, roll up and fasten with skewer or toothpick. Roll in flour and brown in remaining butter. Add 2 cups of water (or meat stock, if you have it) and simmer for 1 1/2 hours. Remove toothpicks. Pour gravy over meat. Garnish with chopped parsley and mashed potatoes.

Pork Chops with Cranberry-Barbecue Glaze

Makes 4 servings

Stir together sauces in a bowl. Grill chops over medium hot coals for 12-15 minutes, turning once. Brush with sauce several times.

"This recipe is from the Wisconsin Pork Producers, which promotes the consumption of both pork and cranberry products produced in Wisconsin. This simple-to-prepare recipe is one that requires very little preparation time for today's busy schedules."
Cynthia Wills
Wisconsin Folklife Festival Participant
Pig showing
Belmont

1/2 c. barbecue sauce

1/2 c. whole berry cranberry sauce

four 1 1/2- inch thick boneless center-cut pork loin chops

Vicki Tzougros
Mother of George Tzougros, Wisconsin Arts Board
Executive Director
Madison

3 large onions, chopped

oil

4 boxes (each 10 oz.)frozen chopped
    spinach, thawed and well-drained

salt and pepper

chopped fresh dill or dried dill weed

1 large carton of cottage cheese

4 eggs, beaten

1/4 - 1/2 lb. feta cheese, crumbled

1/2 c. freshly grated Parmesan cheese or
    more to taste

melted butter

phyllo dough, thawed according to pack-
    age instructions

Spanakopita (Spinach Pie)

Sauté onion in oil until soft. Add spinach and
salt, pepper and dill to taste. Cook a few minutes. Cool. Stir in cottage cheese, eggs, feta,
and Parmesan.

Heat oven to 325 F. Line a 10-by-15-inch cookie
pan with 6 buttered layers of phyllo dough.
Spread filling over dough. Cover with 6 sheets of
buttered phyllo. Bake until golden.

Home-Cured Beef Tongue

Make 3/4-inch cuts across tongues in several places. Mix together salt, sugar and salt peter. Rub mixture well into tongues. Put in covered dish or plastic bag in icebox and turn everyday for 2-10 days. Drain, rinse and place in saucepan with remaining ingredients. Cover with water and bring to simmer. Add bay leaf, peppercorn, cloves and onion. Cook until tender (meat should pierce easily with a fork). Remove, cool, and peel tongues.

Slice thin to serve. Eat warm or cold.

"Eighty years ago, during the winter at the Town Line Cheese factory east of Gratiot, Wisconsin in Lafayette County, my father, a cheesemaker, would have a butchering day for the farmers after the cheese making season. On a December day the farmers would bring their cattle and hogs to the cheese factory. Father would fire up the boiler and the butchering would begin. My mother, Elizabeth, would use every part of the cow from the tail to the moo. This is our Bussman family recipe for home cured beef tongue which tastes like sugar cured ham."
John Bussman
Wisconsin Folklife Festival Participant
Cheesemaker
Monroe

2 beef tongues

1/4 lb. salt

1 t. sugar

1 t. salt peter

1 bay leaf

2 cloves

8 peppercorns

1/2 medium onion

"I have found that restaurants often use carrots, celery or pickle as a filling. They are all very good, but my favorite is still the bacon and onions, also known as "pigs in a blanket." My earliest recollection of this recipe is in my childhood during the 1930's and 1940's. As an adult, I have at times used diced mushrooms as a filling because my grandfather and I both liked them so much. He really enjoyed my mushroom rouladen because he never ate anything my grandmother made with mushrooms. His rationale was based on an old European mushroom joke."

Elfrieda Haese
Wisconsin Folklife Festival Participant
Haese and Sclei, Austrian Music
Colgate

2-3 lb. thin round steak

salt and pepper

mustard

2 medium onions, diced

about 3/4 lb. bacon, chopped

flour

beef broth or water, or a combination of both

1 T. beef bouillon or Kitchen Bouquet

1/2 c. flour mixed with a little water to make a paste (optional)

Rouladen

Lightly season round steak with salt and pepper. Pound steaks with edge of saucer to flatten as much as possible, to 1/4-inch or less. Cut meat into roughly shaped rectangles, about 3 1/2 by 5 inches. Thinly spread pieces with mustard. Place about 2 tablespoons each diced onion and bacon on each slice of meat and roll up. Tuck in edges and tie with string. (String is used because toothpicks can perforate intestines. True story.) Roll lightly in flour and brown in hot, greased skillet. Add beef broth or water (or a combination) to cover along with bouillon or Kitchen Bouquet. Simmer until meat is tender, adding water or broth if needed as it cooks. Remove meat. Thicken the simmering gravy with flour paste, if desired.

Chicken Paprika

Sauté chicken pieces and onions in oil until chicken is tender.

While chicken is cooking, make dumplings: Mix flour and 2 teaspoons salt with eggs. Drop mixture one tablespoon at a time into boiling water. Boil 10-20 minutes. Dumplings will rise to the top when they are cooked. Drain completely.

When chicken is tender, add paprika and salt to taste. Stir in dumplings and add a little water to make more gravy. Simmer briefly, then remove from heat and add sour cream. Serve with additional sour cream.

"This is a family recipe that comes from my father's side of the family. His mother taught my mother to make this dish. It's a traditional recipe from Czechoslovakia. It is also a popular Hungarian dish, which is not surprising considering that my relatives are from the part of Slovakia that is near the Hungarian border. This dish is a favorite family meal that we usually eat for Sunday family dinners or when family members visit."
Cynthia Kerchmar
Wisconsin Folklife Festival Presenter
Illinois

Chicken:

3-5 lbs. chicken pieces

1 large onion, chopped

1 T. oil

1 t. salt

2 T. paprika

1/2 c. sour cream Dumplings:

2 c. flour

2 t. salt

4-5 eggs

Also: additional sour cream

Pam Walker
Wisconsin Folklife Festival Participant
Cranberry Grower
Wisconsin Rapids

1 pre-cooked Italian bread shell

1/4 c. whole-berry cranberry sauce

1 green onion, white and green parts
    sliced

1/3 heaping c. shredded Monterey Jack
    cheese

4 thin slices of deli-style smoked turkey

Smoked Turkey and Cranberry Gourmet Pizza

Makes 1 serving

Preheat oven to 375 F. Place bread shell on an ungreased baking pan. Spread cranberry sauce evenly over bread shell. Sprinkle with green onions and cheese. Top with turkey. Bake for 10 minutes or until cheese has melted. Cut into quarters.

Connie Mahairas
Wisconsin Folklife Festival Participant
Icon painter
La Crosse

Filling:

2 pkg. (each 10 oz.) frozen, chopped
    spinach, thawed

1 medium onion OR 1 bunch green onions,
    finely chopped

1 can (15 1/2 oz.) tomato sauce (or about
    2 cups)

1/2 of a 6-oz can tomato paste

5 eggs

6-8 oz. Feta cheese, crumbled

1 cup grated Parmesan or Romano cheese

1-2 T. dried mint

salt and pepper to taste

Also:

1 lb. phyllo dough, thawed according to
    package directions

1 lb. butter, melted (or more as needed)

Spanakopitas

Makes 50-60 small pastries

To prepare filling:

Squeeze all water from spinach and place in a
mixing bowl. Add finely chopped onions, tomato sauce, tomato paste, eggs, cheese, mint, salt
and pepper. Mix together well by hand and set
aside.

To fill and phyllo dough:

Cover a baking sheet with aluminum foil or
parchment paper. Before opening phyllo package, assemble the following: sharp knife, pastry
brush, aluminum foil, damp towel (wring it out
well), prepared baking sheet, spinach filling,
and melted butter. Open package and unfold
phyllo dough stack and place on dry work surface (short side facing you). Cut stack into thirds
(lengthwise) with sharp knife. Cover with foil and
then cover again with a damp towel.

Uncover one stack of dough. Place a single
sheet of phyllo dough on dry work surface in
front of you (short end towards you). To prevent
dough from drying out, re-cover the stack (or
work very quickly). Lightly brush single sheet of

dough with butter. Place 1 tablespoon of filling in lower left hand corner. Take filled corner and fold in triangle to the right. Keep folding to the left and right as you fold up the pastry into a triangle (as you would fold a flag). Place folded pastry on prepared baking sheet. Brush with more butter. Continue with remaining phyllo dough and filling. Place pastries fairly close together on baking sheet, usually four triangles together.

To bake pastries:

Heat oven to 350 F. Bake pastries until golden brown, about 30 minutes. Remove from baking sheet immediately and place on serving platter. Serve hot.

Diane DeFoe
Wisconsin Folklife Festival Participant
Basket maker
Bayfield

2 c. wild rice

1 t. salt

4 tablespoons (1/2 stick) butter

12-16 ounces fresh mushrooms, sliced

1 medium sweet yellow onion, sliced thin

1 lb. Italian sausage, either hot or mild
   (approximately 5 sausages)

1 pkg. Lipton Onion Soup mix or beef broth

Wild Rice with Italian Sausage

Soak wild rice for two hours in water. Drain. In sauce pan, bring 10 cups water to boil. Add 1 teaspoon salt. Add rice to boiling water, cover and lower heat. Cook rice gently for 20 minutes. Drain.

Heat oven to 350 F. Heat butter in large skillet; add mushrooms and onions. Sauté until delicately brown. Transfer vegetable to Dutch oven. Cut sausages into bite-size chunks and brown well in the skillet. Add sausage to the Dutch oven along with any of the pan drippings. Also stir in the cooked rice, the Lipton soup mix and a cup of water. Toss lightly together and bake until heated through, approximately 20-30 minutes. Rice will not be mushy and the dish ends up moist and crunchy.

Pijani Saran (Drunken Carp)

Heat oven to 350 F. Wash and clean carp, leaving it whole. Season with salt. Refrigerate for 2-3 hours. Stuff the fish with the onion and garlic. Spread oil all over fish (or dip fish in the oil) and sprinkle with pepper. Place the fish in a deep baking dish and bake 45-60 minutes. While the fish is baking, baste frequently with the wine. Garnish with paprika before serving.

"Don't drive after enjoying this meal!"
Stephanie Lemke
Wisconsin Folklife Festival Participant
Croatian egg decorator
Mazomanie

1 whole carp, about 3 lbs.

salt and pepper to taste

1/4 c. onion, finely chopped

2 T. chopped garlic

1/4 c. oil

2 c. white wine

paprika

Stephanie Lemke
Wisconsin Folklife Festival
Croatian egg decorator
Mazomanie

Cabbage:

2 large cabbage heads

Filling:

11/2 c. chopped onion

1 T. butter

1 lb. ground pork

1 c. ham, chopped

1 lb. ground beef

2 eggs, beaten

4 cloves garlic, minced

3 T. chopped parsley

1 T. salt

1/2 c. long grain brown rice

Sauerkraut:

1 can (48 oz). can sauerkraut

Sauce:

4 T. butter

1/2 c. flour

1/2 c. chopped onion

1 T. paprika

1 can (6 oz.) tomato paste

3 c. broth (beef, chicken or vegetable) or
water

Sarma
(Stuffed Cabbage and Sauerkraut)

Cabbage: Fill large pot 1/3 full and bring to boil. Meanwhile, remove cores from 2 large cabbages and put them in boiling water for 5 minutes. Remove from water. Cool.

Prepare filling: Sauté onion in butter until brown. Let cool. Combine with meats, eggs, garlic, parsley, salt and rice in bowl. Mix with hands until well blended. Put aside.

Open canned sauerkraut. Put 1/3 of can in bottom of large pot and spread evenly. Take cooked head of cabbage and carefully peel off leaves (about 20 leaves). Take 1/3 cup of meat mixture and form with hands into sausage shape. Place the "sausages" on cabbage leaves, close to the bottom of core end, and wrap up like a cigar, tucking in ends. Lay in pot on top of sauerkraut, seam side down. Layer with more kraut and continue until all cabbage-meat leaves are in the pot. Layer top with remaining sauerkraut.

Sauce: Melt butter, add flour; stir constantly over low heat until golden brown. Add onion, paprika and tomato paste, stirring between after each addition. Slowly pour in broth or water while stirring until mixture is smooth. Cover and simmer over low heat 3 hours. Top with sour cream. Let stand 15 minutes before serving.

Willi Kruschinski
Wisconsin Folklife Festival Participant
Boat builder/lure maker
Winchester

3 lbs. chopped onions

4-6 T. plus 1/2 c. (1 stick) butter, divided

boneless beef round, sliced through the
    entire round into plate-size,

1/4-inch-thick slices

salt and pepper

waxed paper

mustard

2 lbs. lean bacon, uncooked

dill pickles, quartered lengthwise

white sewing thread

1 c. vegetable oil

oxtail, optional

pickle juice

cornstarch

Rouladen
(Stuffed Rolled Beef Slices)

Makes about 20 rouladen

Have the butcher cut the beef round into 1/4-inch slices, not strips, but rather each one the size of a medium-size plate. You'll need 20-24 slices total.

Sauté the chopped onions in 4-6 T. of butter until well wilted and reduced in volume.

Lay one slice of beef on a piece of waxed paper and sprinkle with salt and pepper to taste. Spread a thin layer of mustard on the slice. To complete the filling, add 2 strips of the bacon, a pickle quarter or two, and 2-3 table-spoons of fried onions, spreading the ingredients the length of the piece of meat. (Use another piece of meat if you need, in order to cover the length of the meat.)

If you don't have a perfect round, don't worry. Roll from the widest side. It should be 7 to 8 inches long when rolled. Wrap with white sewing thread every 4 inches for the length of the roll. Heat half of the remaining butter and oil togeth-er in large skillet; add the rouladen and brown them well. Add more butter/oil as needed. Place them in a large pot with water to almost cover the meat. To increase the flavor, you can add oxtail to the liquid as the rouladen are cooking. Cover and simmer for at least 2 1/2 hours. When they are finished, take the rouladen out of the liquid and cool them for about 1/3 hour. Remove the thread when they are cool. Gravy: To the liquid that the rouladen was cooked in, add any leftover onion and a few spoonfuls of pickle juice. Boil it down if there is too much water. Remove the oxtail. Thicken with cornstarch.

Debra Usinger (recipe from "A friend of Usinger's")
Wisconsin Folklife Festival Participant
Sausage making and cookery
Milwaukee

1 cut-up chicken

1/2 t. salt

1/8 t. pepper

1 T. salad oil

6 Usinger's Fresh Italian sausage links

1 can (28 oz) whole tomatoes, drained
    (save 1/2 c. liquid)

1/2 c. dry red wine

1 c. sliced onions

2 medium green peppers, sliced

1 t. dried basil

pinch of sugar

1/2 t. fines herbs

1/2 t. Italian seasoning

1/2 t. oregano

11/2 c. fresh mushrooms, sliced

1/3 c. flour dissolved in 3 T. water

Italian Chicken

Makes 6 servings

Sprinkle chicken with salt and pepper. Heat oil in large heavy Dutch oven. Cook chicken until lightly browned on all sides (do this in batches if necessary). Remove chicken and set aside. Prick sausages, add to Dutch oven and brown them. Remove sausages and pour off drippings from pot. Add tomatoes with 1/2 cup reserved liquid, red wine, onions, green peppers, basil, sugar, fine herbs, Italian seasoning and oregano.

Simmer two minutes, scraping brown particles from pot. Add mushrooms and stir well.

Add chicken and sausage. Cover and simmer 45 minutes until tender. Push chicken and sausage aside. Skim off fat.

Mix flour and water until smooth. Stir this into 1/4 cup of the pot juices. Add to pot and cook until sauce bubbles and thickens slightly, a few minutes. Stir until meat is well coated.

Bratwurst A la Vern

Put onions and sauce ingredients in cooker. Add beer and sausage. Heat. Serve hot.

"This sauce is great with any link sausage item. For company, double or triple the recipe."Vernon Abramson
Usinger's employee for 32 years/ Submitted by Debra Usinger/Wisconsin Folklife Festival Partipant
Sausage making and cooking
Milwaukee

2-3 onions, sliced and simmered

10 Usinger's fresh bratwurst, grilled

1 bottle or can (12 oz.) beer

Sauce:

1 c. chili sauce

1 T. Worcestershire sauce

1 c. catsup

2 T. vinegar

1/2 t. salt

2 T. brown sugar

1/2 t. paprika

"I hope you enjoy my old German recipe (Schweinkoteletten mit Knackwurst und Kartoffeln). My grandmother, who was a chef in Germany, was the one who brought it with her many years ago."
Carol Martin Kling
Submitted by Debra Usinger/Wisconsin Folklife
Festival Partipant
Sausage making and cookery
Brown Deer

4 pork loin or rib chops

1 T. vegetable oil

1 medium sized onion, chopped

1 medium sized carrot, chopped

1 stalk celery, sliced

2 sweet pickles, finely chopped

6 oz. Usinger's Knackwurst, 1/4-inch slices

2 T. caraway seeds

1/2 t. salt

1/2 t. pepper

3/4 c. water

3 medium potatoes, cut into 1/8-inch slices

parsley or chives for garnish

Pork Chops with Knackwurst

Makes 4 servings

Trim any excess fat from pork chops. Heat oil in 10-inch skillet until hot.

Cook pork chops over medium heat until brown on both sides (about 5 minutes); remove from pan. Add onion, carrot, celery, pickles and knackwurst to skillet until and cook until vegetables are tender; about 15 minutes.

Arrange pork chops on vegetable mixture; sprinkle with caraway seeds, salt and pepper. Pour water over pork chops. Arrange potato slices on top. Heat to boiling; reduce heat. Cover and simmer until pork chops and potatoes are tender, about 45 minutes. Garnish with parsley or chives.

Breads, Rolls And Muffins...

Wisconsin Through Recipes

Sekahiivaleipa
(Mixed grain loaves)

Sonja Luoma
Wisconsin Folklife Festival
Rag rug weaver
Saxon

Makes 2 loaves

In a mixing bowl, dissolve yeast in the warm water. Add oil, salt, oatmeal and half of the bread flour. Beat with an electric mixer until smooth. Stir in remaining bread flour and other flour with a wooden spoon until the dough forms a ball. Turn onto a floured board and knead until dough is smooth. It will remain somewhat sticky. Put the dough back into the mixing bowl, cover with a kitchen towel and let rise in a warm place for 11/2 to 2 hours, or until double in bulk.

Lightly grease a large baking sheet or line it with parchment paper. Turn dough onto a floured board and knead until smooth. Form dough into two round loaves. Transfer them to prepared baking sheet. Prick loaves all over with a fork, sprinkle them with flour and cover with a kitchen towel. Let them rise in a warm place for about 45 minutes. Heat oven to 375 F. Bake the loaves 30 minutes or until slightly browned and loaves sound hollow when tapped with a finger. Cool on a rack that has been covered with a kitchen towel.

2 envelopes dry yeast

2 c. warm water (110 F)

2 T. vegetable oil or melted butter

2 t. salt

1 c. oatmeal

2 c. bread flour or all-purpose flour

1 c. whole wheat flour

1 c. rye flour

Diana Schroeder
Wisconsin Folklife Festival Participant
Member of the Clete Bellin Orchestra
Manitowoc

Batter:

1 1/2 c. flour

1/2 c. sugar

2 t. baking powder

1 t. cinnamon

1/4 t. salt

1 egg, beaten

2/3 cup buttermilk

1/4 c. (1/2 stick) butter or margarine, melted

Filling:

1 1/2 c. fresh rhubarb cut into small pieces

1/4 c. peach preserves

Topping:

1 T. sugar

1 t. cinnamon

Cinnamon Rhubarb Muffins

Makes 9 muffins

Heat oven to 400 F. Grease nine muffin cups. To make batter: Combine flour, sugar, baking powder, cinnamon and salt in a bowl. In another bowl, combine egg, buttermilk and butter. Stir into dry ingredients just until moistened. Spoon 1 T. of batter into each muffin cup. For filling, combine rhubarb and peach preserves. Place 1 T. in the center of each cup (do not spread). Top with remaining batter.

For topping, combine 1 T. sugar and 1 t. cinnamon. Sprinkle over batter. Bake 20 minutes or until top of muffin springs back when lightly touched in the center.

Irish Soda Bread

Beat egg(s) in a bowl; stir in milk and salad oil. Combine remaining ingredients in separate bowl. Stir the two mixtures together. Oil and flour round pan or cast iron skillet. Spread batter in pan and let stand for 20 minutes. Meanwhile, heat oven to 350 F. Bake bread about 1 hour or until golden brown.

"This is my mom's, Mary McAllister Pryor, recipe for Irish soda bread. She bakes it in a large cast iron skillet, which gives it a great shape and flavor. A slice of the bread is perfect with a cup of tea."
Anne Pryor
Wisconsin Folklife Festival Staff, Program Coordinator for Education and Outreach
Madison

1 or 2 eggs

1 1/2 c. milk

1 t. salad oil

31/2 c. flour

4 1/2 t. baking powder

1/2 t. baking soda

1/2 c. sugar

1 t. salt

1 T. caraway seeds

1 1/2 c. raisins

Rita Horvath
Wisconsin Folklife Festival Staff, Supply Coordinator
Madison

1 pkg. dry yeast

2 c. sour cream

1 T. milk (optional)

5 c. flour

1/2 lb. (2 sticks) margarine, at room tem-
    perature

2 eggs

salt to taste

Pogacsa (Biscuits)

Mix yeast with small amount of sour cream to dissolve. If needed add 1 tablespoon of milk In a big mixing bowl add flour and rest of ingredients, including yeast mixture. Mix together with hands. Cover with cloth and set aside at warm room temperature 1/2 - 1 hour.

Heat oven to 400 F. Flatten dough on table and roll out to 3/4-inch thickness. Cut dough with a cookie cutter or top of drinking glass into rounds. Place on ungreased cookie sheet. Bake 25-35 minutes, or until golden brown. Serve with Hungarian Goulash soup (p.24).

Never Fail Rolls

Mix together milk, sugar and salt. Crumble in the yeast. Stir until dissolved. Stir in rest of ingredients. Mix together and knead lightly. Let rise in warm place until double in bulk. Form dough into rolls and let rise. Bake at 375 F. for 25-30 minutes.

"I remember eating these rolls at Thanksgiving time particularly. They would be hot from the oven and Grandma would tuck them under a clean dishtowel to keep them warm. We always have a lot of different dishes, and have to work to find room to fit everything on the table. One of my favorite Thanksgiving traditions is watching Grandma make the gravy. She pours the flour-water mixture into the drippings, stirs it quickly, and continues. My mom helps out by making these rolls now, but Grandma still makes the gravy."
Kathy Oppegard
Wisconsin Folklife Festival Staff, Assistant Volunteer Coordinator
Madison

2 c. scalded milk (cooled to lukewarm)

1/2 c. sugar

2 t. salt

2 small cakes yeast

2 eggs, beaten

1/2 c. shortening

about 71/2 c. flour

"We used to make the loaves large, about 2 1/4 pounds per loaf. Now we make them smaller.."
Paul "Sugar Bear" Smith
Wisconsin Folklife Festival Participant
Native American agriculturist
Oneida

Ground dry corn or corn"flour":

boiling water

1 quart white flint (Indian) dry corn

1 cup clean wood ash, sifted and large
   chunks removed

Corn bread:

boiling water

finely ground dry corn "flour" from above
   (preparation instructions below)

handful of cooked kidney beans (be con-
   servative about the amount you use)

1 t. salt

ice water

Cannery Corn Bread

Makes 2-3 loaves

To prepare the dry corn for cannery corn bread:

Bring large kettle of water to a rolling boil. Add dry corn kernels to water. Add wood ash. (The purpose of the ash is to "hull" the corn.) When adding the ashes, the tradition is to stir the mixture counter clockwise. Cover pot and boil this mixture until the kernels turn an orangeish color. Keep it at rolling boil, stirring occasionally. Boil the mixture approximately 20-30 minutes, until the kernels turn yellowish again.

After the kernels have cooked, pour the corn into a metal mesh strainer or "specialized" corn washing basket and run them under cold water to rub the corn against the sides to get the corn hulls off. Important Note: This must be done with an outside hose as the lye in the ash will eat away your household pipes. You can tell when the hulls are off by taking the corn kernels and rubbing them through your hands. No hulls should be on your hands after the above process. Please keep in mind that this process takes a very long time.

After the corn is washed, spread the kernels

out in a dehydrator or on your kitchen table with a fan blowing. Leave fan on constantly. If you dry

your corn on the table, occasionally move the kernels to dry them out. The drying process takes 12-24 hours.

Once the corn is dry, you will grind it with by hand with a mortar and pestle or with an electric grinder. You will need approximately 1 quart of dry kernels to equal the amount of ground corn (or "flour") needed to make 2-3 loaves of bread.

To prepare cannery corn bread:

Bring a large pot of water to boil. Mix the corn flour, beans and salt together and make a well in the center of the flour. Gradually add boiling water to the corn flour until the water is absorbed and can be stirred to a "thick cookie-dough" consistency. (Be careful not to mush the kidney beans.) Rub your hands through ice water and, while the batter is still hot, take handfuls of the dough and shape them into round loaves. Loaves should be about 1 pound each.

Using a heavy flat ladle or a board, place each loaf carefully in an upright position in the boiling water. Cover and continue cooking the loaves in a gently rolling boil for approximately 40 minutes, or until the breads float to the top of the kettle. Carefully remove the loaves, draining excess water.

Place the loaves on a flat surface to cool. While bread is cooling, it will firm up enough to slice. A reminder: cornbread has to be refrigerated. It tastes best when warm with butter or honey on it. Enjoy!

Cookies

and
BArs...

Wisconsin Through Recipes

Cookies:

1 c. (2 sticks) margarine

1 c. sugar

1 egg

1/2 c. honey

1/2 c. white corn syrup

5 c. sifted flour

11/2 t. baking soda

1/2 t. salt

2 t. ground ginger

1 t. cinnamon

1/2 t. ground cloves

1/4 t. nutmeg Frosting:

1 lb. white chocolate

1 T. shortening

Sidonka's Slovak Honey Cookies

Cream margarine and sugar. Add egg, honey, and corn syrup. Combine 5 cups sifted flour (sift before measuring), baking soda, salt and seasonings and sift again. Stir dry ingredients into wet ingredients until combined. Divide dough into 3 or 4 sections; wrap in plastic wrap. Chill 6 to 8 hours.

Heat oven to 375 F. Grease cookie sheets. Roll out dough sections one at a time on floured surface to 1/8- or 1/4-inch thickness, depending on the type of cookies. (Larger cookies need more thickness.) Cut out cookies with cookie cutter shapes and bake on prepared cookie sheets until slightly golden, 5 -15 minutes, depending on size of cookie. Because of the honey and syrup in these cookies, they stick if you let them cool too long on the sheets, so remove cookies as soon as possible. Cool them on the side: waxed paper placed over aluminum foil makes a better cooling surface than a cake rack, again to prevent sticking. Cool cookies thoroughly before frosting.

Melt white chocolate in the top of a double boiler. Add 1 tablespoon of shortening. Keep flame or heat low as white chocolate scalds easily. Spread on cookies or fill pastry bag and squeeze out decoration onto cookies.

Viennese Cut-out cookies

Makes about 61/2 dozen cookies

Cream margarine and powdered sugar. Add egg and extracts. Blend in sifted flour (sift before measuring) and salt. Chill 6-8 hours. Heat oven to 375 F. Lightly grease cookie sheets. Roll out dough to 1/8 inch thickness on floured surface. Use a cookie cutter to cut heart shapes into the dough. In half of the hearts, cut out a hole in the center---these hearts will be the cookie tops. (The leftover "holes" may be baked and frosted or filled with jelly.) Place all hearts on prepared sheets and bake 7-8 minutes. Cool thoroughly.

Spread bottom cookies (without holes) with jelly, placing a little more jelly toward the center of cookie. Sprinkle the cookie tops with powdered sugar and place the tops on the bottoms.

Sidonka Wadina
Wisconsin Folklife Festival Participant
Wheat weaver
Lyons

Cookies:

1 c. (2 sticks) margarine

1 c. powdered sugar

1 egg

11/2 t. almond extract

1 t. vanilla extract

21/2 c. sifted flour

1 t. salt

Other

strawberry or currant jelly

additional powdered sugar for sprinkling on cookies

"This recipe only requires a strul iron. I have an electric double iron on which I bake two at a time. The old-fashioned irons were set on the wood stoves or electric burners. These irons were very heavy and easy to get your fingers burned."
Eleanor Bagstad
Wisconsin Folklife Festival Participant
Member of the Norskedalen Trio
Westby

        2 cups whipping cream (whipped until
            very thick)

        3/4 c. sugar

        pinch of salt

        1 t. vanilla

        1 3/4 c. flour

Strul (Waffle Cookie)

Mix all the ingredients together well. Keep dough cool until ready to use. Place a teaspoon of dough on strul iron. Bake just until golden brown. Remove from iron with a knife and roll on a wooden stick. Pull off when cool. If strul sticks to grill, place a little oil on a paper towel and rub onto grill.

Oatmeal Cookies

Heat oven to 375 F. Grease cookie sheets. Mix soda in the milk. Cover raisins with water and bring to a boil. Drain; chop or grind raisins. Mix all the ingredients. Using your hands, form dough into balls slighter larger than a walnut. Then flatten and place on cookie sheets. Bake until golden brown.

"In 1926 I made these cookies in a logging camp. My family and I have been making them ever since."
Dora Henkelman
Wisconsin Sesquicentennial Folk Arts Exhibitor
Merrill

2 t. baking soda

2/3 c. milk

2 c. raisins

1 c. lard

1 c. brown sugar

1 c. white sugar

1 t. salt

2 t. cinnamon

4 c. flour

4 c. oatmeal

1/2 lb. (2 sticks) salted butter

1/2 lb. (2 sticks) unsalted butter

1 lb. dark corn syrup

1 lb. dark brown sugar

1 t. ground cloves

1 t. ground nutmeg

1 t. ground ginger

1 t. ground cinnamon

1 t. dried orange peel, ground

2/3 t. finely ground pepper

7 c. unbleached white flour, divided

1 egg

2 tablespoons sugar

11/2 t. fresh yeast

1 t. baking powder

Optional:

cold coffee

colored sugar and other cookie decorations

Latvian "Piparkukas" (Peppercakes)

Bring butters, corn syrup, dark brown sugar, and all spices (not baking powder) to a boil in a 4-quart non-stick pot. Remove from heat. Sift 4 cups flour and stir into mixture. Let cool.

Beat the egg in a bowl. In separate bowl, stir 2 tablespoons white sugar into the yeast. When dough is cool or almost cold, stir in beaten egg and yeast mixture. Combine the remaining 3 cups flour with baking powder and knead it into the dough. Store dough in a container in a cool, dry location for a couple of days.

Heat oven to 350 F. Roll dough on floured surface to about 1/8-inch thickness Cut with cookie cutters into Christmas shapes. If decorations are desired, moisten tops with cold coffee and sprinkle colored sugar or other decoration on top. Bake 8-10 minutes or until set and light brown. Cookies will be thin and crunchy.

Cranberry Slices

Heat oven to 350 F. Generously grease a 9-by-13-inch baking pan. Beat eggs well and gradually add sugar. Add melted butter and flour continuing to mix until well blended. Fold in nuts and cranberries by hand.

Spread evenly in pan. Bake 30-40 minutes. They are done when they get light brown in coloring. Cool and slice into desired sizes.

"This is a delicious dessert served chilled and topped with a small mound of whipped cream."
Eric Olesen
Wisconsin Folklife Festival Participant
O&H Danish Bakery
Racine

2 eggs

1 3/4 c. sugar

6 oz. (12 T.) butter, melted

1 1/3 c. all-purpose flour

9 oz. (about 2 cups) fresh cranberries

3/4 c. chopped pecans

"The original recipe used 1 cup of lard and 1 cup of butter. This is a recipe I have had for practically 40, 50, 60 years."
Selma Spaanem
Wisconsin Folk Arts Exhibitor
Mt. Horeb

1 c. (2 sticks) butter, at room temperature

1 c. (2 sticks) shortening, at room temperature

1 c. sugar

1 egg

4 c. flour

pinch of salt

1/2 - 1 t. vanilla extract or other flavoring

Sandbakkelse

Makes about 7 dozen cookies

Heat oven to 350 F. Cream butter, shortening and sugar. Add egg. Then add flour, salt and flavoring. Mix well. Press into ungreased sandbakkelse tins (they look like ruffled muffin tins). I use regular muffin tins. Bake until lightly brown.

Belgian "Boonohs"

Cream butter in large bowl with wooden spoon. Gradually add the sugars, creaming all the while. Beat in eggs, vanilla, and salt. Stir in flour until a stiff dough forms (less flour makes crispier cookies). Cover bowl and chill dough overnight.

Roll chilled dough between the palms of your hands into small balls about the size of a marble. Keep extra dough balls cold (we used to place them in pie pans and refrigerate them) as you bake the cookies in a well-heated, fine grid Belgian cookie iron* until golden brown. The amount of time will depend on how hot the iron is, and how cold and dense the dough is. If you use a stove-top iron (as opposed to an electric one), flip the grid half-way through baking to brown the cookies on both sides. Cool thoroughly on wire racks. Store airtight.

*Note: You may not have an heirloom Belgian cookie iron, but you can use an electric one. Unlike the stove-top iron, the electric version makes two cookies at a time, and while they don't seem to come out quite as crisp and thin as ones made in our heavy, flame-heated iron, they come mighty close. You can purchase an electric Belgian cookie iron from C. Palmer Manufacturing, Inc., P.O. Box 220, West Newton, PA 15089, 412-872-8200. Be sure to ask for Model #1110, which has the smallest grids.

"Nothing makes me feel more Belgian than a "boonoh" during the holidays. My family bakes these small waffle-like cookies one at a time in the blackened, turn-of-the-century iron one of my paternal grandparents "brought over" long ago. A modern Flemish-Belgian cookbook calls the cookies wafeltjes, but my clan, who originated in the French-speaking southern part of Belgium (Wallonia), uses a nickname that was probably based on a French or Flemish word for "good." Boonohs, then, are "goodies," as my father explained to us. He explained to us, too, exactly how boonohs should look, taste and be prepared. The hand rolled balls of dough are the size of a large marble. The iron is well-heated, the heavy grids flipped by a long handle--just once!--for each cookie. The finished product is golden in color, not too thick, and buttery-good.
This batch makes several dozen cookies, but my family often made two batches, enough to fill a 5-gallon cherry tin that we then stored in the fruit cellar throughout the holiday season. When we'd had our fill of eating them "straight," we'd make ice cream sandwiches out of them."
Terese Allen
Madison

> 1 lb. butter, softened
>
> 11/2 c. white sugar
>
> 1 c. light brown sugar
>
> 8 eggs, well beaten
>
> 1 t. vanilla extract
>
> pinch of salt
>
> 6-7 cups flour

Desserts and pastries...

Wisconsin Through Recipes

Sidonka Wadina
Wisconsin Folklife Festival Participant
Wheat weaver
Lyons

Strudel dough:

3 c. all-purpose flour

1 whole egg

1 t. sugar

pinch of salt

1 t. melted pure lard

1 c. lukewarm water

a little melted butter

a little flour Apple filling:

31/2 lbs. cooking apples, peeled, cored,
and sliced thin

1 2/3 c. granulated sugar tossed with 1 t.
cinnamon

1 c. bread crumbs, toasted to a light brown
color in 3 tablespoons melted

butter

1 c. ground walnuts

º lb. raisins (optional) Also:

flour to sprinkle over tablecloth

approximately 3/4 lb. (21/2 to 3 sticks) butter, melted

Bratislava Apple Strudel

To make strudel dough: Sift flour into bowl. Add egg, sugar, salt, lard and warm water. Knead well until dough is very smooth and soft. Roll dough into a ball and brush with butter and a little flour. Place the dough on a floured cloth in a deep bowl; fold cloth over dough to cover it. Let stand for 1 hour. Meanwhile measure and prepare filling ingredients as described in list of ingredients (but do not mix them together).

To stretch and fill dough, and bake strudel: Heat oven to 375 F. Lightly grease baking pan(s). Spread a tablecloth on a table and sprinkle with flour. Remove dough from the bowl and gently place dough in the center of the tablecloth. Butter top of dough with warm, melted butter. Butter your hands. Place hands under dough and work slowly and gently to stretch the dough from the center. Work round and round the table stretching the dough. When the dough starts to become thin, stretch with the backs of the hands, palms down. Stretch the dough until it completely covers the table; it should be at least 3 feet by 4 feet or larger. When the dough is stretched large enough, it will be as thin as tissue paper.

Cut away the thick edges. Sprinkle entire surface with melted butter. Leaving a 2-inch border all around, layer on the filling ingredients in the order they are listed: apples, sugar/cinnamon, bread crumbs, walnuts and raisins (if desired). Sprinkle the filling with melted butter. Lap side edges over about 2 inches and fold the end of the dough nearest you over the filling. Now with both hands, raise the cloth and the strudel will roll itself. Cut the roll to fit the size of the baking pan(s). Brush with melted butter, place in prepared pan(s) and bake approximately 1 hour or until golden brown.

Easy Low-fat Microwave Norwegian Rommegrot

Melt butter in microwave, add flour and stir until smooth. Scald milk, add to butter/flour mixture and stir until smooth and somewhat thickened. Heat the "grot" in microwave for additional 1-1 1/2 minutes. Stir in 1/4 cup sugar. Sprinkle each serving with a little sugar, butter pieces, cinnamon and a few raisins. Serve it and enjoy.

Phillip Odden/Else Bigton
Wisconsin Folklife Festival Participants
Norwegian wood carvers
Barronett

1/2 c. (1 stick) butter

2/3 c. flour

1 scant quart milk

1/4 c. sugar

additional sugar

additional butter, cut into pieces

cinnamon

raisins

"Very easy and one of Phil's favorites."
Phillip Odden/Else Bigton
Wisconsin Folklife Festival Participants
Norwegian wood carvers
Barronett

11 oz. skin-on almonds, ground (for extra
    flavor, almonds may be toasted before
    grinding them)

3 eggs

11 oz. sugar

1 T. unbleached flour

1 t. baking powder

whipped cream blended with chocolate
    syrup to taste

Nottekake (Nut Cake)

Heat oven to 350 F. Grease and flour a 10-inch
springform cake pan. Mix first five ingredients.
Pour into prepared pan. Bake about 45 minutes
(should be crusty on outside and a bit chewy on
inside). Cool. Top with chocolate flavored
whipped cream.

"You'll need a set of round kransekake baking rings for this towering special-occasion cake. The rings are graduated in size and are available at Scandinavian specialty shops and kitchen supply stores. You should have 6 forms, each with 3 circles, to make 18 cake rings total. The rings are baked, glazed and then stacked. Lykke til!"
Phillip Odden/Else Bigton
Wisconsin Folklife Festival Participants
Norwegian wood carvers
Barronett

Kransekake Cake:

1 lb. almonds

1 lb. powdered sugar

2-3 level t. flour

3-4 egg whites

bread crumbs or uncooked "Malt-o-meal" cereal
    Glaze:

1 egg white

2-3 drops vinegar

7 oz. powdered sugar

Norwegian Kransekake (Norwegian Almond Ring Cake)

Make sure the almonds are dry. Grind the almonds. Mix with powdered sugar and flour. Add 3 egg whites first, working them in by hand and not with a mixer. Add more egg white if needed. The dough should be firm but not dry.

Heat oven to 400 degrees. Grease forms and sprinkle insides of each circle with bread crumbs or Malt-o-meal. Roll dough into long, 1/2-inch-thick rope-like pieces. Cut the pieces to length to fit into the forms. Pinch the ends together inside the forms to make a tight seam. Bake on the middle rack in the oven 10-12 minutes. Cool the cakes down fast (you can put them outside in the winter or in the freezer or refrigerator in the summer). When cake rings are cold, remove them from the forms.

To make glaze: Stir together the egg white, vinegar and powdered sugar to make a thick glaze. Use a pastry bag with a thin-holed decorating nozzle and make a zig zag pattern over top surface of each ring (some may drizzle down the sides). Assemble the cake by stacking the rings when the glaze is dry. Store the assembled cake in an airtight container. A peeled potato or piece of bread can be put in the box a couple days before the cake is served. This will keep it chewy. Eat the cake by pulling off the bottom rings, one at a time, and breaking them into pieces.

Rich Coffee Cake and Filling

Phillip Odden/Else Bigton
Wisconsin Folklife Festival Participants
Norwegian wood carvers
Barronett

To make pastry: Mix flour, butter, sugar, and salt as for pie crust. Dissolve yeast in warm milk then add to the flour mixture. Add egg yolks or eggs. Mix well. Cover. Let rise in warm place until double in bulk.

Meanwhile, make filling: Mix crushed graham crackers, melted butter, brown sugar, vanilla or almond extract, and almond paste (if desired) to make filling.

To form and bake pastry: Heat oven to 375 degrees. Grease one or two large baking pans or line them with parchment paper. Divide dough into 3 portions. Roll out or pat on floured board to 3/4-inch thickness, each portion about 6 inches wide and 10 inches long. Spread each one with filling and roll up in jelly roll fashion. Form each roll into a round ring. Pinch ends together. Slit outside top of ring with scissors at 1-inch intervals all around (the slits should be about an inch long; they will spread open as the cake bakes). If desired, you may give a little turn to each slit opening (for more attractive look). Place on prepared pan(s) and let rise in warm place until double. Bake 20-25 minutes. Drizzle still-warm cake with powdered sugar icing.

Pastry:

3 c. flour

1 c. butter

4 T. sugar

1 t. salt

1 pkg. dry yeast

1 c. warm milk

4 egg yolks or 2 whole eggs

Filling:

18 graham crackers, crushed

1/4 to 1/2 c. melted butter

1/2 c. brown sugar

2 t. vanilla or almond extract

1/2 c. almond paste (optional)

Also: powdered sugar icing

"Flan is traditionally made in a special mold called a flanera. This mold has a lid and very small handles. If you don't have anything like this, an 8-inch stainless steel saucepan (non-metal handle removed) works just as well."
Rosa Chavez
Wisconsin Folklife Festival Participant
Day of the Dead Altar maker

Caramel:

1/2 to 3/4 c. sugar

Custard:

1 can (14 ounces) sweetened condensed milk

1 can milk (measure milk in the same can that sweetened milk comes in. Use any kind of milk you like)

1 t. vanilla extract

4 eggs

Also:

raspberries, strawberries, or other berries

Easy Flan

Makes 8 servings

Pour one inch of water into a metal mold (deep pie pan) and place on the bottom rack of oven. Heat oven and pan of water at 350 F. at least 10 minutes before proceeding with the recipe.

To prepare caramel: Place sugar in flanera or 8-inch stainless steel saucepan (handle must be heat-proof). Heat over medium-low flame, and stir with a wooden spoon. Sugar will begin to melt and turn light yellow to light brown. When all the sugar is melted and is light brown (take care! sugar burns easily), remove from heat. Quickly rotate the saucepan in order to coat bottom and sides while the caramel is hot. Set aside to cool.

To prepare custard: Pour milks and vanilla into blender; blend on high speed. Slowly add eggs one by one. Pour this mixture into caramelized saucepan and cover with aluminum foil. Place flan mold into the bigger mold with water. Bake for approximately 1 hour or until toothpick inserted in center comes out clean. Cool completely. Loosen with a spatula. Carefully invert onto a platter. Chill in refrigerator. Serve cold or at room temperature. Garnish with berries.

Flan Variations:

Traditional Flan:

5 c. milk
1 c. sugar
6 eggs
1 t. vanilla

Heat milk and sugar. Beat eggs. Very slowly add milk to eggs, and continue to beat until frothy. Beat in vanilla. Caramelize the mold and cook flan the same as Easy Flan.

Light Flan:

Substitute the richer ingredients with low-fat or non-fat sweetened condensed milk; skim milk; and 5 egg whites and two yolks, OR 2 eggs and egg substitute equal to remaining eggs.

Flavor Substitutes:

Instead of using vanilla, try one of the following: pine nuts, shredded coconut, grated lemon rind (grate the yellow part only), etc.

Eggs:

Recipes vary greatly when it comes to eggs. Some call for more eggs, and others use less. In some recipes, only yolks rare used. If you like a firmer texture, use more eggs. If you're watching your cholesterol, use more egg whites and less egg yolks or use part egg substitute. There's plenty of room for experimentation!

Rich Cheese Flan:

1 package (8 oz.) cream cheese, at room temperature
1 can (14 oz.) evaporated milk
1 can (14 oz.) sweetened condensed milk
1 t. vanilla extract
4 eggs

Follow same procedures as for Easy Flan (blending cream cheese with other ingredients).

Fast Flan:

Try using a pressure cooker. Add about 6 inches of water to cooker; place a pie pan upside down in cooker. Cover filled mold securely with aluminum foil and/or metal lid. Put mold on top of the pie pan to avoid getting water inside. Place lid on pressure cooker and add the valve. Place over high heat. Once steam comes out strongly and the valve starts to whistle, turn down the flame a little. The flan is done in about 20 minutes. Cool. Open pressure cooker and remove mold. Proceed as usual.

Individual Flan:

Individual glass molds can be used. To avoid cracked molds, heat glass molds in the microwave before pouring caramel inside. Use just a little caramel on the bottom of the mold. Proceed as usual.

10 eggs, separated while cold, then bought to room temperature

14 T. sugar (about 1 cup)

6 oz. bittersweet or semi-sweet chocolate, melted slowly over hot water and cooled

2 c. finely chopped (not ground) walnuts

Passover Chocolate Cake

Makes 8-12 servings

Heat oven to 350 F. Beat the egg yolks and sugar until very thick and lemon-colored. Stir in the chocolate. Fold in the nuts. In clean bowl, beat the egg whites until stiff but not dry. Fold into the chocolate-nut mixture. Turn into a greased 10-inch springform pan. Bake 1 hour or until the center springs back when lightly touched with the fingertip. Cool in the pan on a cake rack.

Chocolate Bundt Cake

Heat oven to 350 F. Grease and flour a bundt cake pan. Combine cake mix, pudding mix, sour cream, oil, eggs, and warm water in large bowl. Beat 4 minutes. Stir in chocolate chips. Pour into prepared pan. Bake 50-60 minutes, then turn cake out onto a wire rack. Cool completely. Sprinkle with powdered sugar. Serve with whipped cream or Cool Whip, if desired.

"This is my family's favorite chocolate cake. It is very moist even without frosting. This cake is often made for special occasions such as birthdays or other parties."
Pat Ehrenberg
Wisconsin Folklife Festival Participant
Quilter from Sew Happy Quilters
Ripon

  1 box (18.5 oz.) chocolate or devil's food cake mix

  1 package (3 æ oz.) instant chocolate pudding mix

  1 c. sour cream

  1/2 c. cooking oil

  4 eggs

  1/2 c. warm water

  11/2 c. semi-sweet chocolate chips

  powdered sugar

  whipped cream or Cool Whip (optional)

"My recipe came from my mother, but the same recipe is in the Coon Valley ALCW cookbook. I would guess it goes back to grandma's time. It goes real good with a cup of coffee. It can be made for any occasion."
Beatrice Olson
Wisconsin Folklife Festival
Member of the Norskedalen Trio
Westby

3 eggs

11/4 c. sugar

1/4 c. (4 tablespoons) melted butter

1 c. buttermilk

1 t. vanilla extract

4 c. flour

2 t. baking powder

1 t. baking soda

1/2 t. salt

lard or Crisco oil for deep-frying

Doughnuts

Makes about 3 dozen doughnuts

Beat eggs thoroughly. Beat in sugar and melted butter. Stir in buttermilk. Stir in vanilla. In a separate bowl, sift together flour, baking powder, baking soda and salt. Add to the egg and buttermilk mixture. Chill dough at least 1 hour. Roll or pat out dough about 1/3-inch thick. Cut with doughnut cutter. Heat lard or oil in deep-fat fryer to 350 F. Fry doughnuts a few a time. Drain on paper towels.

Point Bock Beer Cake

Heat oven to 350 F. Grease and flour a 9-by-13-inch pan. Cream shortening and sugar. Add beaten eggs and melted chocolate. Stir in flour, baking soda, beer and sour milk; mix until smooth. Stir in cherries, cherry juice and chopped nuts. Spread in prepared pan. Bake 40 minutes. Cool. Frost with your favorite frosting.

Geri Zappa
Wife of John Zappa
Wisconsin Folklife Festival Participant
Beer brewing
Stevens Point

2/3 c. shortening, at room temperature

2 c. sugar

2 eggs, beaten

2 squares unsweetened chocolate, melted

21/2 c. flour

2 t. baking soda

1 c. Point bock beer

3/4 c. sour milk (add 2 teaspoons vinegar or lemon juice to milk and let stand a few minutes)

1 small jar maraschino cherries, drained (reserve 1/4 cup of the juice) and chopped

1/2 c. chopped nuts

frosting of your choice

Sour Cream Pie

Heat oven to 350 F. Mix dry ingredients together in a heavy saucepan. Rinse the raisins and add to the dry ingredients. Add the vanilla and sour cream. Boil until mixture thickens, stirring often to prevent scorching. Pour filling into pie crusts. Bake approximately 40 minutes or until golden brown.

"This recipe was given to me by my mother, who in turn received it from her mother. This recipe is soon a century or more old."
Eleanor Bagstad
Wisconsin Folklife Festival Participant
Member of Norskedalen Trio
Westby

3/4 c. sugar

2 T. flour

1 scant t. cinnamon

1/2 t. salt

1 c. raisins

1 t. vanilla extract

1 c. sour cream

2 unbaked pie crusts

Nodji's Cranberry Tassies

Makes 2 dozen

To make crust, cream the cream cheese and butter until well blended. Stir in flour until dough forms. Chill 1 hour. Shape into 1-inch balls. Mold into ungreased miniature muffin tins.

To make filling and bake: Heat oven to 325 F. Beat egg, brown sugar, butter, vanilla, and salt until creamy. Divide nuts evenly into the bottom of the crusts. Do the same with chopped cranberries. Add filling (not to exceed the edge of the crust). Bake about 25 minutes or until filling is set. Cool in pans.

"This is a special dessert prepared for special family occasions. I especially make this dessert at Christmas time. Many times I give these cranberry tassies as a gift to such individuals as teachers, the mailman, elderly people in the area, etc."
Nodji VanWychen
Wisconsin Folklife Festival Participant
Cranberry grower
Warrens

Crust:

1 small pkg. (3 oz.) cream cheese, softened

1/2 c. (1 stick) butter, softened

1 c. sifted flour (sift before measuring)
Filling:

1 egg

3/4 c. packed brown sugar

1 T. butter

1 t. vanilla extract

dash of salt

2/3 c. coarsely broken pecans

1 c. chopped fresh cranberries

"This is a recipe from my mother-in-law. She made this pie for me when I first met her some 25 years ago. She will always make this for me on my birthday and other special occasions. She always says the pie is so good because "I" grew the cranberries."

James VanWychen
Wisconsin Folklife Festival Participant
Cranberry grower

2 c. cranberries, cut in half

1/2 c. brown sugar

1/2 c. chopped walnuts

1 pie crust for 10-inch pie pan

2 eggs

1 c. sugar

1 c. all-purpose flour

1/2 c. (1 stick) butter or margarine, melted
    ice cream

Jim's Favorite Cranberry Pie

Heat oven to 400 degrees. Combine cranberries, brown sugar and walnuts. Spread mixture in the bottom of the prepared pie crust. In a medium mixing bowl, beat eggs well. Gradually add sugar while you continue beating. Stir in flour and melted butter or margarine. Pour batter over the berries. Cover edges of pie crust with foil and bake 15 minutes. Reduce heat to 350 F., remove foil and bake at 35 minutes longer. Serve with ice cream.

Streusel Raspberry-Cherry Pie

Prepare pastry for a single 9-inch pie crust as directed on package. Flute edges. Do not prick or bake.

Heat oven to 425 F. Combine remaining pie crust mix with brown sugar, nuts and cinnamon in mixing bowl. Drain raspberries and cherries; reserve liquid. Combine sugar and cornstarch in saucepan. Add 3/4 cup reserved liquid. Mix well. Cook over medium heat, stirring constantly until mixture boils and is thick and clear. Stir in drained raspberries and cherries. Pour into pastry-lined pan. Sprinkle crumb mixture over fruit. Bake 10 minutes. Reduce oven temperature to 350 F. and continue baking pie 20-25 minutes, until golden brown.

"This is my step-mother's recipe, Peggy Rice. She makes it mostly in the summer time for special occasions, with fresh cherries that we picked on our vacation in Door County. When we lived in Stevens Point we had raspberry bushes, and she would use fresh raspberries too."
Megan Rice
Wisconsin Folklife Festival Staff, Graphic Design Intern
Madison

1 pkg. Betty Crocker pie crust mix (2 crusts)

1/2 c. firmly packed brown sugar

1/4 c. chopped nuts

1/2 t. cinnamon

1 package (10 oz.) frozen raspberries, thawed

1 can (1 lb.) sour pie cherries

2/3 c. sugar

3 T. cornstarch

3/4 c. liquid drained from raspberries and cherries

"The minimum of 32 layers of dough folded over butter is what makes Danish pastry. This is what is different from just a sweet dough. To make kringle correctly is virtually an all-day project at home. For the best results, you cannot deviate from the procedure."

Ray Olesen, father of Eric Olesen
Wisconsin Folklife Festival Participant
O&H Danish Bakery
Racine

Dough:
11/2 sticks (3/4 cup butter), softened
1 package (2 ounces) cake yeast
1/4 cup warm water
1/4 cup lukewarm milk
1/4 cup sugar
1/2 teaspoon salt
1/2 teaspoon lemon extract
1 egg
2 cups sifted all-purpose flour Butterscotch
    filling:
1 cup brown sugar
1/3 cup butter, softened
pinch of salt
pinch of cinnamon
1/2 egg white
Other:
chopped nuts, fruit, or jam for filling
11/2 cups powdered sugar for icing

O & H Danish Kringle

To make dough: Trace or mark an 8-inch square in pencil on each of two pieces of waxed paper. Divide softened butter in half and spread each half evenly over the marked squares. Chill to harden the butter. While butter is chilling, break up yeast, place in large bowl, and stir in 1/4 cup warm water until yeast is dissolved. Add the 1/4 cup lukewarm milk, sugar, salt, lemon extract, and egg; mix well. Stir in flour until dough is smooth.

Turn dough (it will be soft and sticky) onto well-floured surface. Sprinkle with flour and knead it very lightly and briefly, about 3-4 turns. Roll out dough to an 8-by-12-inch rectangle with floured rolling pin. Place one of the chilled butter squares over the bottom two-thirds of dough; peel off waxed paper. Fold the top, uncovered third of dough over the middle third, then fold the remaining third over the top of the fold. Now, working from the right side of the dough rectangle (instead of the top), again fold one end over the middle third of dough, and fold remaining third over the fold, making a square of nine layers. Flour lightly and wrap in waxed paper. Chill 30 minutes.

Roll out dough again to an 8-by-12-inch rectangle. Place second square of chilled butter over dough as before and again do the folds as described above, to make a square of 18 layers. Flour lightly, wrap in waxed paper, and chill 2 hours.

Meanwhile, make butterscotch filling by mixing ingredients until smooth. Line two baking pans with parchment paper or aluminum foil.

After dough has chilled a second time, cut it in half. On floured surface, lightly roll out each piece to a 20-by-6-inch rectangle. Spread half of the butterscotch filling lengthwise down the middle third of each rectangle, then spread your choice of nuts, fruit, or jam over the filling. Fold one of the long edges to the center of filling. Moisten other long edge and fold over the top to completely cover filling. Press along seam to seal well. Place each folded rectangle, seam side up, on a prepared baking sheet and form into oval shape, pressing ends of kringle together to close the circle. Flatten kringles with your hand, cover with light cloth or plastic wrap, and let rise in warm (70-degree) place for 1 hour.

Heat oven to 350 degrees before dough completes its rising. Bake kringles until golden brown, 25-30 minutes. Cool in pans on wire racks.

Combine powdered sugar with 2 tablespoons water; beat until smooth. Spread icing over cooled kringles. It's also nice to decorate the kringles with chopped nuts or fruit. Kringle keeps very well in the freezer or for several days in the refrigerator. The high butter content keeps them moist.

Stephanie Lemke
Wisconsin Folklife Festival Participant
Croatian egg decorator
Mazomanie

Filling:

1 medium can crushed pineapple

2 T. cornstarch

1/2 c. sugar

1 t. lemon juice

Dough:

1/2 lb. (2 sticks) butter, softened

1/2 c. sugar

3 c. flour

2 t. baking powder

1 t. salt

1/2 t. baking soda

1/4 pint sour cream

4 egg yolks

Also:

powdered sugar

Pita iz Ananasa (Pineapple Pita)

Combine all filling ingredients in saucepan and cook until thickened. Cool.

To make dough: Cream butter and sugar. Add dry ingredients, sour cream and egg yolks. Mix and refrigerate for about 1/2 hour. Heat oven to 350 F. Pat half the dough into a 9-by-13-by-2-inch baking pan. Add filling. Roll or pat out remaining dough and fit over filling; prick top crust before baking. Bake 40-45 minutes. When done, sprinkle with powdered sugar

Ida Denzin's Kuchen

Heat oven to 350 or 375 degrees. Mix all dough ingredients except milk and egg in a bowl. Mix milk and egg in separate bowl, then combine the two mixtures. Press mixture into a 13-by-9-by-2-inch pan. Add sliced fruit in horizontal rows. Mix streusel ingredients with fork and sprinkle over filling. Bake 30-45 minutes, until lightly brown.

"My grandmother Emma Manke gave me this recipe. It was her mother, Ida Denzin's, recipe. She brought it to Milwaukee from Stetton, Germany in the 1860's. My aunt and their cousins still use this recipe. I make this kuchen with seasonal fruit."
Chris Manke
Wisconsin Arts Board Staff, Percent for Arts Coordinator
Madison

Dough:

2 1/2 c. flour

1/2 c. sugar

1 T. butter

1 T. shortening

1/4 t. salt

3/4 c. milk

1 egg

Fruit:

approximately 3 cups lightly sugared, sliced fruit such as rhubarb, peaches, plums, etc.

Streusel:

1 c. flour

1/2 c. sugar

cinnamon to taste

Sidonka Wadina
Wisconsin Folklife Festival Participant
Wheat weaver
Lyons

Dough:

3 c. all-purpose flour

1/2 lb. butter, at room temperature

1/4 t. salt

1 package (8 oz.), at room temperature

3 T. sugar

1 t. baking powder

1 t. vanilla extract

1 egg yolk

2 T. water

For work surface and for rolling dough:

sugar

Filling:

1 package (8 oz). cream cheese

Rosky-Filled Crescents

Makes 3 1/2 - 4 dozen

Sidonka uses Philadelphia brand cream cheese for this recipe.

To make dough: Combine flour, butter, salt and cream cheese in a bowl. Mix on low speed until blended. Add sugar, baking powder, vanilla, egg yolk and water. Mix together. Turn pastry out on pastry board and knead. Divide dough into 2 balls. Wrap in plastic wrap and refrigerate overnight or 8 hours.

To form and bake pastries: Let dough stand at room temperature 15-20 minutes before rolling it out. Meanwhile, heat oven to 375 F. Grease two cookie sheets. Place dough in center of pastry board that has been sprinkled with white granulated sugar. Roll dough out into a rectangle. With pasty cutter, cut rectangle into 2-by-2 1/2-inch pieces, about 3 1/2 - 4 dozen pieces total. Cut cream cheese into small pads that are about 1-by-1 1/2-inches in diameter and about 1/4-inch thick. Place a pad of cream cheese on each dough piece. Roll the long end over and around the cream cheese, being careful to keep the cream cheese in the center. Lightly pinch ends shut to keep the cheese from squishing out as you roll the dough. Roll each pastry in additional sugar just to coat lightly. Shape into a horseshoe and place seam side down on baking sheets. Bake on center rack of oven, one sheet at a time, for about 20-25 minutes. When the tops of the cookies are just slightly golden, remove from oven and immediately cool on wax paper-covered aluminum foil. Tastes best when slightly warm.

Cranberry Pie

Makes 8 servings

Heat oven to 325 F. Grease a 10-inch pie plate. Sprinkle cranberries, 1/2 cup of the sugar and the walnuts over the bottom of the pie plate (in that order). Beat eggs until yolks and whites are thoroughly combined. Add remaining 1 cup sugar, melted butter, sour cream and sifted flour. Beat until dry ingredients are just moistened. Pour batter over the cranberry layer. Bake 1 hour until the top is golden brown.

Pam Walker
Wisconsin Folklife Festival Participant
Cranberry grower
Wisconsin Rapids

2 c. fresh cranberries

1 1/2 c. sugar, divided

1/2 c. walnuts

2 eggs

1/2 c. (1 stick) butter or margarine, melted

1/4 c. sour cream

1 c. all purpose, sifted

Stephanie Lemke
Wisconsin Folklife Festival Participant
Croatian egg decorator
Mazomanie

Dough:

4 packages dry yeast

3 t. sugar plus 1 c. sugar, divided

1/2 c. milk, warmed

1/2 lb. (2 sticks) butter, at room temperature

3 large eggs

1 c. sour cream

1 t. vanilla extract

1 t. salt

7 c. flour

Filling:

12 c. ground walnuts

2 1/4 c. sugar

1/2 c. (1 stick) butter, at room temperature

1 can (20 oz.) pineapple bits, not drained

1 T. vanilla extract

1 t. grated lemon rind (grate yellow part only)

milk, if needed

Also:

4 tablespoons butter

1 egg (optional)

Orahnjaca (Nut Roll)

Heat oven to 350 F. Generously grease cookie pans. To make dough: Combine yeast, 3 t. of the sugar and the warm milk; stir and set aside. Cream remaining 1 cup sugar with butter well. Add eggs one at a time. Add sour cream and vanilla. Add 1 cup of flour at a time. If you need more flour, add 1 tablespoon at a time, kneading until the dough is smooth and no longer sticky. Divide dough into 6 balls. Place balls in plastic bags to keep them soft.

Combine filling ingredients in a bowl. Add only enough milk to make filling spreadable.

To form and bake pastries: Roll out one ball on a floured surface into a 12-by-14-inch rectangle. Spread dough with about 1 1/2 cups of the filling. Roll up. Seal ends by clamping and turning ends under. Repeat procedure with 2 more balls. (If you have a large oven, you can do all 6 balls at once. If not, bake 3 at a time, keeping the remaining dough covered and warm, and punching it down as needed.) Place rolls on prepared pans (not close together). Melt 4 tablespoons butter and brush with melted butter. Set aside in warm place for 1 hour until double in bulk. Bake in preheated 350-degree oven for 45-55 minutes. If you'd like, make an egg wash by beating 1 egg with 2 tablespoons water. Brush top of rolls with egg mixture and return to oven for 5 minutes.

Photo Descriptions

cover and xiv   One of the women at Mineral Point's First Methodist church displays a tray of pasties. Photo courtesy of Bob Rashid.

title page   Irene Vuorenmaa and Governor Tommy Thompson in the Foodways Demonstration area at the Smithsonian Folklife Festival. Photo courtesy of Bob Rashid.

i   One of the visitors at the Smithsonian Folklife Festival enjoys a piece of watermelon. Photo courtesy of Bob Rashid.

3   Cheesemaker Bill Schlinsog talks to visitors at the Smithsonian Folklife Festival. Photo courtesy of Bob Rashid.

iv   Preparing lefse for the annual lutefisk dinner served at the Lakeview Lutheran Church in Madison. Photo courtesy of Anne Pryor.

13   A woman prepares lefse at the Lakeview Lutheran Church in Madison. Photo courtesy of Anne Pryor.

v   A man stirs booyah at an annual parish dinner in Tisch Mills, Wisconsin. Photo courtesy of Andy Kraushaar.

21   Betty Lacapa and Fred Benjamin sort through wild rice after it has been parched. Photo courtesy of Bob Rashid.

26   Paul "Sugar Bear" Smith examines an ear of corn at Tsyuhekwa, the sustainable agriculture-based farm at Oneida. Photo courtesy of Barbara Lau.

30   A man stirs booyah at an annual parish dinner in Tisch Mills, Wisconsin. Photo courtesy of Andy Kraushaar.

vi   Dorothy Hodgson makes pasties at the Foodways Demonstration area at the Smithsonian Folklife Festival. Photo courtesy of Bob Rashid.

vii   Members of the Lakeview Lutheran Church prepare meatballs for their annual lutefisk dinner. Photo courtesy of Anne Pryor.

viii   Both lutefisk and Swedish meatballs are served at this annual lutefisk dinner in Black Earth. Photo courtesy of Andy Kraushaar.

ix   A father and son help to prepare the lutefisk for the annual lutefisk dinner in Black Earth. Photo courtesy of Andy Kraushaar.

45   Visitors at the Smithsonian Folklife Festival observe a pasty making demonstration. Photo courtesy of Bob Rashid.

47   The members of Mert Cowley's deer hunting camp relax at the table after a delicious meal of venison. Photo courtesy of Andy Kraushaar.

61   Andy Tranel of the Walker Cranberry Company shows how cranberries are harvested with a hand rake. Photo courtesy of Ruth Olson.

71   Racks of roasting chickens serve the many guests at the Waterloo Fourth of July celebration in Firemen's Park. Photo courtesy of Anne Pryor.

x   Sorting lutefisk for the annual lutefisk dinner served at the Lakeview Lutheran Church in Madison. Photo courtesy of Anne Pryor.

xi   The Foodways Demonstration area at the Smithsonian Folklife Festival. Photo courtesy of Bob Rashid.

xiii   A Green Bay Packers cake, served at a tailgate party at Lambeau Field, before the Packers-Cowboy game. Photo courtesy of Andy Kraushaar.

xv   Pasty making in the Foodways Demonstration area at the Smithsonian Folklife Festival. Photo courtesy of Bob Rashid.

91   Alice in Dairyland, Courtney Ott, demolishes a cream puff at the Wisconsin State Fair. Photo courtesy of Andy Kraushaar.

100   Two women display the pies available at the annual Hunter's Supper in Dairyland, Wisconsin. Photo courtesy of Andy Kraushaar.

105   Eric Olesen makes kringle in the Foodways Demonstration area at the Smithsonian Folklife Festival. Photo courtesy of Bob Rashid.

Editor: Terese Allen:

Wisconsin native Terese Allen is a former professional cook. She currently pursues her love for food through writing. Allen is the author of "The Ovens of Brittany Cook Book," "Fresh Market Wisconsin," "Wisconsin Food Festivals," and most recently "Hometown Flavor," a book that highlights specialty markets, bakeries, butcher shops and cheese factories throughout Wisconsin.

Recipes compiled by: Choua Ly:

Choua Ly recently earned her Bachelor of Arts degree in Behavioral Science & Law and Sociology from the University of Wisconsin-Madison. She joined the Wisconsin Folklife Festival staff in January of 1998; she will be pursuing her Juris Doctor at the University of Wisconsin Law School in August 1998.

Graphic Design and Layout: JoAnn Blohowiak

JoAnn Blohowiak recently earned her Bachelor of Arts degree from the University of Wisconsin Green Bay in Studio Art, Humanistic Studies and Graphic Communication. She is an intern for the Wisconsin Arts Board, hired specifically to design this project.

Home Cooked Culture: Wisconsin Through Recipes is produced as part of the Wisconsin Folklife Festival. The Wisconsin Folklife Festival is produced by the Wisconsin Arts Board in association with the Smithsonian Institution and the Wisconsin Sesquicentennial Commission. Corporate contributors include AT&T, SC Johnson Wax, and The Credit Unions of Wisconsin.

WISCONSIN

ARTS

BOARD